THE BASICS

At a time of unprecedented interest in Stoicism, this book offers a comprehensive introduction to Stoic ethics for students and for readers interested in Stoic life-guidance.

It combines an explanation of the main philosophical ideas in ancient Stoic ethics by Christopher Gill with discussion of how to put these ideas into practice in our own lives by Brittany Polat.

The first seven chapters examine central Stoic ethical claims and the questions raised by their claims, including:

- Why does our happiness in life depend solely on virtue?
- Is ethics grounded on nature; and, if so, does this mean human nature or the natural world?
- What is the connection between gaining ethical understanding and relating properly to other people?
- What counts as right action and how do we learn to make good decisions?
- What is the proper place of emotion in the good life?

The two final chapters discuss the significance of these Stoic ideas for modern thought, especially for virtue ethics and environmental ethics, and the Stoic contribution to guidance on living.

With a glossary of key terms and suggestions for further reading, *Stoic Ethics: The Basics* is an ideal starting point for anyone looking for an accessible and lively explanation of Stoic ideas and their implications for practical living.

Christopher Gill is Emeritus Professor of Ancient Thought at the University of Exeter, UK, following earlier appointments at Yale, Bristol and Aberystwyth Universities. He has published many books and articles on ancient philosophy, especially Stoicism. These include *The Structured Self in Hellenistic and Roman Thought* (2006), *Marcus Aurelius: Meditations Books 1–6, translated with an introduction and commentary* (2013) and *Learning to Live Naturally: Stoic Ethics and its Modern Significance* (2022).

Brittany Polat holds a PhD in applied linguistics but is currently devoted to the study and practice of Stoicism. As a philosophical writer, speaker and community organizer, she specializes in conveying complex philosophical ideas in a form that is accessible to a wide and diverse audience. Her most recent book is *Journal Like a Stoic: A 90-day Program to Live with Greater Acceptance, Less Judgement, and Deeper Intentionality* (2022).

THE BASICS

The Basics is a highly successful series of accessible guidebooks which provide an overview of the fundamental principles of a subject area in a jargon-free and undaunting format.

Intended for students approaching a subject for the first time, the books both introduce the essentials of a subject and provide an ideal springboard for further study. With over 50 titles spanning subjects from Artificial Intelligence to Women's Studies, *The Basics* are an ideal starting point for students seeking to understand a subject area.

Each text comes with recommendations for further study and gradually introduces the complexities and nuances within a subject.

BIOETHICS (SECOND EDITION)	**CRITICAL THINKING (SECOND EDITION)**
ALASTAIR V. CAMPBELL	*STUART HANSCOMB*
EASTERN PHILOSOPHY (SECOND EDITION)	**GLOBAL DEVELOPMENT**
VICTORIA HARRISON	*DANIEL HAMMETT*
PHENOMENOLOGY	**FOOD ETHICS (SECOND EDITION)**
DAN ZAHAVI	*RONALD SANDLER*
ATHEISM	**PERCEPTION**
GRAHAM OPPY	*BENCE NANAY*
EMOTION	**PHILOSOPHY OF TIME**
MICHAEL BRADY	*GRAEME FORBES*
PHILOSOPHY OF MIND	**CAUSATION**
AMY KIND	*STUART GLENNAN*
METAPHYSICS (SECOND EDITION)	**PHILOSOPHY OF LANGUAGE**
MICHAEL REA	*ETHAN NOWAK*
FREE WILL (SECOND EDITION)	**STOIC ETHICS**
MEGHAN GRIFFITH	*CHRISTOPHER GILL AND BRITTANY POLAT*

Other titles in the series can be found at:
https://www.routledge.com/The-Basics/book-series/B

STOIC ETHICS

THE BASICS

Christopher Gill and Brittany Polat

Routledge
Taylor & Francis Group

NEW YORK AND LONDON

Designed cover image: © Getty Images

First published 2025
by Routledge
605 Third Avenue, New York, NY 10158

and by Routledge
4 Park Square, Milton Park, Abingdon, Oxon OX14 4RN

Routledge is an imprint of the Taylor & Francis Group, an informa business

© 2025 Christopher Gill and Brittany Polat

The right of Christopher Gill and Brittany Polat to be identified as authors of this work has been asserted by them in accordance with sections 77 and 78 of the Copyright, Designs and Patents Act 1988.

All rights reserved. No part of this book may be reprinted or reproduced or utilised in any form or by any electronic, mechanical, or other means, now known or hereafter invented, including photocopying and recording, or in any information storage or retrieval system, without permission in writing from the publishers.

Trademark notice: Product or corporate names may be trademarks or registered trademarks, and are used only for identification and explanation without intent to infringe.

ISBN: 978-1-032-81357-8 (hbk)
ISBN: 978-1-032-81359-2 (pbk)
ISBN: 978-1-003-49937-4 (ebk)

DOI: 10.4324/9781003499374

Typeset in Bembo
by codeMantra

CONTENTS

Preface   ix

    Introduction: Opening the door to Stoic ethics   1
1 Does happiness depend only on virtue?   11
2 How does virtue relate to other values?   27
3 Is Stoic ethics grounded on nature?   40
4 How do we learn to be good?   55
5 How do we learn to make good decisions?   71
6 How do we learn to have good emotions?   87
7 How should we relate to other people and society?   103
8 What does Stoicism contribute to modern virtue ethics and life-guidance?   118
9 What does Stoicism contribute to modern environmental ethics?   134

Glossary   149
References   154
Index   157

PREFACE

This book provides an introduction to Stoic ethics. All quotations are in English and the writing is intended to be readily accessible. We have in mind especially the needs of two kinds of reader. One kind consists of students doing undergraduate courses in degree programmes such as Philosophy or Classics/Classical Studies. The other kind consists of general readers who are interested in Stoicism as a basis for living, especially those who have read, for instance, one or two 'life-guidance' books or translations of Epictetus and Marcus Aurelius and who want to go more deeply into Stoic ethical ideas. The book is also meant to be helpful and interesting to any other kind of reader who wants an introduction of this kind.

Each chapter (after the introductory chapter) consists of two parts. The first and longer part, by Christopher Gill, is a discussion of an important aspect of Stoic ethical theory. The second, shorter part, by Brittany Polat, headed 'Modern Applications', discusses the same topic in a more informal way, and considers how we might apply this Stoic theme in our own lives. Some readers might prefer to read the applied sections first and then come back to the more detailed preceding treatment.

The book is arranged in this way. Chapters 1–3 examine certain distinctive ideas which are fundamental for Stoic ethics in general.

Chapters 4–7 explore other important concepts in Stoic ethics; ethical development or learning is an underlying theme. Chapters 8–9 explore the implications of Stoic ethics for modern thought of different kinds. References in this book such as 'see Chapter 1' or 'Chapter 4, p. 00', with a capitalized C, are to other chapters in the book or to chapters and pages.

Each chapter is followed by 'Further Reading'. First, we list one or two other general books on Stoic ethics. Then, for more advanced students or those with access to university libraries or similar resources, we list some scholarly books or articles, along with ancient writings relevant for the topic of the chapter. There are also brief endnotes in most chapters, with references to ancient writings or scholarly works. Finally, in most chapters, we also list some widely available books on the practical application of the relevant Stoic ideas.

Two books which provide the core ancient evidence for Stoic ethics are referred to throughout the book by initials:

IG = B. Inwood and L. P. Gerson, *The Stoics Reader: Selected Writings and Testimonia*, translated with introduction (Indianapolis: Hackett, 2008).

LS = A. A. Long and D. N. Sedley, *The Hellenistic Philosophers* (Cambridge: Cambridge University Press, 1987).

Note also: *NE* = *Nicomachean Ethics*, by Aristotle.

For more information on translations of ancient writings on Stoic ethics, see the Further Reading after the introductory chapter, 'Opening the door to Stoic ethics'. All modern scholarly works in the endnotes cited by author and date are given in full in the References at the end of the book.

We are grateful to Julia Annas for reading two sample chapters and giving us helpful and thoughtful advice on the format and presentation of the book. Thanks also to Gareth Jones for reading these chapters and for his positive comments. Special thanks are due to Tom Schmid for extensive and penetrating comments on a previous version of the introductory chapter and Chapters 1–3. We are also grateful to two anonymous readers for further detailed suggestions and to Andrew Beck, Philosophy Editor at Routledge, for his support and advice.

INTRODUCTION
Opening the door to Stoic ethics

This introductory chapter begins by offering what can be called an overall 'vision' of Stoic ethics, which highlights key features and unifying themes. The chapter continues by summarizing distinctive features of Stoic ethics and outlining the place of Stoicism in ancient ethical theory. It concludes by discussing the ancient writings that provide the main primary sources for Stoic ethics. The Further Reading includes details on translations of these ancient writings that may be useful for readers of this book.

THE 'VISION' OF STOIC ETHICS

Stoic thinkers have distinctive and innovative ideas on the main topics and issues for debate recognized in ancient ethical philosophy. Stoicism also offers an overall 'vision' of ethics, connecting these ideas to each other, and providing the basis for putting the theory into practice in one's life. The following summary presents key features of this vision, which are set out here in the same order as they are discussed in Chapters 1–7. It concludes by highlighting the actual or potential contribution of Stoic thought to specific areas of modern ethical debate and practice, which forms the subject of Chapters 8–9.

DOI: 10.4324/9781003499374-1

Fundamental to this vision is the idea that our happiness in life depends on us ourselves, as agents, and not on circumstances or the things we acquire or lose. The Stoic teacher Epictetus conveys this idea with his repeated message that we should focus on what is 'up to us' or what we can control, and not on 'externals'. Happiness does not depend on health, property, or even the welfare of our family and friends, even though these are things that we all naturally want to have. It depends on whether or not we use our agency to develop the virtues and use these to shape our lives. Happiness depends *solely* on this, and not partly, as some other ancient philosophers maintained. The Stoics bring out this idea by a striking contrast between two terms. Virtue and the happiness based on virtue are *good* (they benefit us unconditionally and they are what really matters in life), whereas things such as health and property are '*indifferents*', which may or may not benefit us and which are not what really matters in life. The correct use of indifferents depends on whether we have and exercise virtue.

The claim that our happiness depends on us might give the impression that Stoic ethics is individualistic or subjective in approach; however, this impression would be misleading for several reasons. For one thing, virtue (Greek, *aretē*), conceived as a unified set of virtues (wisdom, courage, justice, temperance or moderation) is seen as forming a type of knowledge or expertise in living. Developing virtue is not a matter of subjective self-expression but is more like learning a practical skill, with definite methods and objective content.

Also, the Stoics do not regard happiness (*eudaimonia*) as just a state of mind or mood (which is a typical modern view) but as a way of life, which affects all aspects of living, including emotions. Happiness is often defined in Stoicism as 'the life according to virtue' or 'the life according to nature' (which are seen as the same thing). The way of life based on virtue is conceived as being in line with the best qualities of human nature, or those of the natural world, in so far as they form part of human life. This point implies another distinctive Stoic feature and a potential contribution to modern thought. 'Nature' is conceived as a richer and more ethically significant type of reality than is often supposed in modern science.

What are the qualities of human nature and the natural world that we should aim to develop in our own lives? In broad terms, human nature at its best is conceived as combining rationality and sociability. The best qualities of the natural world include structure, order, wholeness and consistency; and these are also characteristics of virtue and happiness based on virtue. The natural world also embodies patterns which underpin types of care that are fundamental for human life: care for oneself and for others of one's kind. These ideas form part of the objective content of the Stoic conception of happiness as a way of life. Conceiving human and universal nature in this way can serve to expand our conception of what virtue and happiness involve.

The Stoics believe that all human beings are essentially capable of developing virtue and happiness based on virtue. Ethical development does not depend on having a special kind of inborn nature, social habituation and intellectual education, as some other ancient thinkers supposed. Ethical development can take place in and through activities that form part of virtually any human life such as practical decision-making and forming relationships with others.

This type of development is presented as progress towards a combination of gaining ethical understanding and forming well-judged relationships with other people. A key part of ethical understanding is recognition of the goodness of virtue (and happiness based on virtue), by contrast with the value of 'indifferents'. Well-judged relationships with other people are those guided by virtue as a mode of expertise in living. These relationships can be with members of one's family or community. Human beings as a whole are also seen as forming a community of rational and sociable animals and as proper objects of care for other human beings. Thus, ethical development is a matter of learning a skill, and has objective content, including knowledge of what it means to be properly human.

A key part of Stoic thinking about ethical development is their theory of 'appropriation' (*oikeiōsis*). The Stoics regard it as natural for human beings to 'appropriate' or 'own' their character as rational and sociable animals, capable of developing virtue and happiness, and also to 'appropriate' other human beings, who share this character. Although the Stoics see ethical development as a 'natural' process in these senses, they also acknowledge that completion of this process (that is, achieving perfection in virtue and happiness) is a rare and exceptional achievement. For virtually all of us, the most we can attain is making progress towards virtue through the pathways of ethical development. However, the life of progress is still worthwhile and is a valid expression of our human nature and our ethical agency.

Stoic thinking on these core subjects (virtue, happiness, indifferents, nature and ethical development) forms the basis for the rest of their ethical theory. This theory includes their ideas on ethical decision-making, emotions, and interpersonal and social relationships. Virtue as expertise in living determines whether or not these factors form part of a good human life and make for happiness.

Thus, in making decisions about appropriate actions, it is not enough just to carry out social obligations or duties, taken on their own. We need also to consider how, and whether, these obligations can be fulfilled in a way that expresses the virtues. Proper decision-making also involves (in Stoic terms) 'selection of indifferents', such as health, property, and welfare of family and friends) in a way that is in line with the virtues and with human nature at its best. Though we may not achieve perfection in virtue in this respect, we should aim to make progress in decision-making of this kind.

Ethical development, for the Stoics, is not a purely rational or intellectual process, but one that involves all aspects of our psychological life, including our emotions and desires. The Stoics distinguish between 'emotions' (or 'passions') based on misguided ethical beliefs and 'good emotions', which express ethical understanding and virtue. What the Stoics call the 'therapy' or cure of misguided emotions is brought about by progress in ethical understanding and in properly conducted relationships with others.

The Stoics regard engagement in family, friendship and community as part of a full human life and they place a positive value on other-benefiting actions and attitudes. They stress that our concern for others should be extended to those affected by our actions who fall outside our family and social or political context but who form part of the community of humankind. However, they also stress that what is needed for proper engagement in relationships is not just the desire to benefit others but also virtue as expertise in living. They also emphasize that virtue is properly expressed in taking care of oneself as well as others, and do not see care of oneself and care of others as being in competition with each other. Both forms of care can form part of a virtuous life and one that is 'according to nature' in the Stoic sense.

As brought out in the preceding outline, Stoic thinkers have original and powerful ethical ideas, which add up to a coherent philosophical 'vision', set out here in Chapters 1–7. In Chapters 8–9, we explore the contribution of these ideas to specific areas of modern ethical thought and practice. The main area where Stoic ethics has already made a substantial contribution is what is often called 'life-guidance' (discussed in Chapter 8). This contribution has drawn on the exceptional resources of ancient Stoic writings on ethical guidance and the management of one's life, taken alongside Stoic thinking on the psychology of emotions.

However, we argue that the Stoic ethical ideas presented here are also well-placed to have significant influence on two other areas. These are modern virtue ethics, discussed in Chapter 8, and environmental ethics, especially regarding our response to climate change, considered in Chapter 9. The main features of Stoic ethics relevant for all three areas consist in their thinking on virtue, happiness and other types of value, and their innovative theory of ethical development conceived as 'appropriation'. Also important, especially for virtue ethics and environmental ethics, is the close linkage established between ideas of virtue or happiness and ideas of nature, both human nature and environmental or cosmic nature. These points of connection illustrate that the 'vision' of Stoic ethics is not only important in the context of ancient ethics but has a continuing resonance and force for modern thought.

DISTINCTIVE FEATURES OF STOIC ETHICS

Before placing Stoic ethics in the context of ancient theory more generally, it is worth highlighting three general characteristics of the Stoic approach.

In comparison with most other ancient ethical theories, Stoic ethics is marked by a high degree of internal coherence and unity, and a systematic, worked-out character. This is a characteristic not just of Stoic ethics, but Stoic philosophy in general. For instance, Stoic thinkers aim to combine and integrate the three main branches of philosophy (logic, ethics and physics or theory of nature) in a cohesive and systematic way.

A second distinctive feature of Stoic ethics is a striking combination of ethical rigour or idealism and a broadly naturalistic outlook.

While arguing for what were seen in antiquity as rigorous and idealistic ethical claims, they also insist that their ideas are consistent with the realities of human nature and, indeed, with the natural world more generally. This implies a richer and broader conception of 'nature' than is often assumed in modern scientific thought.

A third characteristic is Stoic interest in the practical application of their ethical theory, and the close integration of theory with practice. Stoicism is exceptionally rich in writings offering guidance on putting ethics into practice in different areas. However, such writing is not considered as merely 'applied ethics', without theoretical content, but rather as an extension of theory in a practical direction. This close linkage between theory and practice is underlined in this book; hence, most chapters combine analysis of Stoic theories with a section on putting this theory into practice.

STOICISM WITHIN ANCIENT ETHICS

How should we locate Stoic thought in the context of ancient ethical theory?

The first Greek philosopher who focused on ethics was Socrates (469–399 BCE). Socrates conducted his philosophy in oral discussions; the early dialogues of Plato are generally seen as giving a reliable picture of Socratic thought and method. Plato (427–347 BCE) followed Socrates in regarding dialogue as the primary mode for philosophical activity. His philosophical works are written in dialogue form; many of these writings centre on ethical questions, including the *Republic*, his most famous work. Aristotle (384–322 BCE) started as Plato's pupil and wrote widely on all aspects of philosophy. He was the first thinker to define the scope and limits of ethics and to write works explicitly devoted to that subject, notably the *Nicomachean Ethics*.

There is a good deal of common ground between the ethical concerns of Socrates, Plato and Aristotle. The central topics are the nature of happiness, assumed to be the goal (in Greek, *telos*) of life, or what matters most in life, virtue, and the relationship between virtue and happiness. Also important is the psychological basis of virtue and happiness (that is, ethical motivation and emotions), ethical development, and interpersonal or social ethics (*philia*, 'friendship' or interpersonal bonding). Stoic ethical theory is also centred on these questions.

However, the Stoics put forward original and distinctive ideas on all these subjects, which do not rely on the ideas of previous thinkers.

Although Socrates had many followers, he did not set up his own school of philosophy. However, both Plato and Aristotle did. Although these were described as 'schools' with 'heads', they were still relatively informal groups of friends engaging in philosophical discussion. They met in public places in Athens; the Academy (the site of Plato's school), and the Lyceum (Aristotle's school) were public gymnasia with open space around them.

Zeno, founder of the Stoic school (334–262 BCE), lectured in the painted Stoa or colonnade near the centre of Athens (hence the name 'Stoics'). There were several competing philosophical schools in this period, including the Epicureans, who met in the large garden of Epicurus' house outside Athens. The ideas Zeno put forward in his lectures and books were extended, elaborated and modified by successive heads of the school and by other Stoic thinkers throughout the third and second centuries BCE. This was the most philosophically creative phase of Stoicism; it falls within the period of Greek history known as 'Hellenistic' (roughly the third to the first century BCE).

Chrysippus, the third head (approximately 280–206 BCE), was the major theorist of the school, wrote many treatises, and did much to give Stoic theory its systematic character. The later summaries of Stoic ethics seem to be largely based on his writings. The last head was Panaetius (185–110 BCE). The school was based at Athens, the centre of Greek philosophical life, until the late second century BCE. Following Rome's conquest of Athens (86 BCE), Stoic thought was more widely spread, with Rome providing the main focus. Stoicism remained active and influential in this more diffused form until the end of the second century CE.

ANCIENT STOIC WRITINGS ON ETHICS

The writings of the Stoic thinkers in the third and second century BCE (the most creative part of the history of the school) have all been lost and are known only through later quotations or summaries. The most important sources are two summaries of Stoic ethics from two much later handbooks. These are by Diogenes Laertius (third century CE) and Stobaeus (fifth century CE), the latter summary, apparently, based on Arius Didymus (first century BCE). Also important is Book 3 of Cicero's *On Ends* (first century BCE), which forms part of a review of Hellenistic ethical theory. Despite their late date, we believe that these sources accurately reflect Hellenistic Stoic ideas, especially those of Chrysippus. These three summaries of Stoic ethics form the main basis of evidence for the present book. They are also the sources most quoted in modern scholarly sourcebooks or accounts of Stoic ethics.

Cicero (106–43 BCE), though not himself a Stoic, is a valuable source for Stoicism. In addition to *On Ends* 3, especially important are his *On Duties*, offering Stoic guidance on practical deliberation, *Tusculans*, Books 3–4, on emotions, and *The Nature of the Gods*, Book 2, on the Stoic worldview. Seneca (1–65 CE) was a committed Stoic who wrote extensively on ethics, in writings that bridge Stoic theory and its practical application, including his *Letters* and many essays and dialogues.

The sources noted so far seem to be closely based on the theories of the heads of the Stoic school in the Hellenistic period. Rather different in kind are two other Stoic works from the early Roman Empire. *The Discourses* of Epictetus (roughly 50–130 CE) are reports of discussions by a well-known Stoic teacher, with key extracts in the *Handbook*. The *Meditations* of Marcus Aurelius (121–189 CE) is a private philosophical notebook by a Roman emperor, rediscovered and published long after his death.

Both works offer an independent formulation of core ethical teachings. They focus on Stoic ideas which have clear implications for the way we should live our lives. In recent years, these works have been very widely used for 'life-guidance'; and they do, indeed, offer powerful statements of central Stoic ethical messages. However, it is not easy to determine precisely how close their contents are to the Hellenistic ethical teachings which form the primary subject of this book. They are generally quoted here to illustrate the practical application of Stoic ideas rather than as the main primary sources for Stoic ethical doctrines.

FURTHER READING

Two short accessible overviews of Stoic ethics:

B. Inwood, *Stoicism: A Very Short Introduction* (Oxford: Oxford University Press, 2018); ch. 5.

J. Sellars, *Stoicism* (Chesham: Acumen, 2006); ch. 5.

For more advanced study, with access to university libraries:

J. Annas, *The Morality of Happiness* (Oxford: Oxford University Press, 1993), covers ancient ethics generally, but includes several chapters on Stoicism.

B. Inwood (ed.), *The Cambridge Companion to the Stoics* (Cambridge: Cambridge University Press, 2003), chs. 1–2 are on the history of Stoicism, and ch. 9 is on ethics.

B. Inwood and P. Donini, 'Stoic Ethics', in K. Algra, J. Barnes, J. Mansfeld and M. Schofield (eds), *The Cambridge History of Hellenistic Philosophy* (Cambridge: Cambridge University Press, 1999), 675–738.

Translations of ancient Stoic writings (most of the books listed here are available in recent, affordable paperbacks):

The most useful single book, including all or part of the three key ancient summaries of Stoic ethics, is:

B. Inwood and L. P. Gerson, *The Stoics Reader: Selected Writings and Testimonia*, translated with introduction (Indianapolis: Hackett, 2008), pp. 113–95 on ethics, pp. 58–85 on theology (or worldview). This is referred to as 'IG' throughout this book.

Most of the same ancient writings are also in B. Inwood and L. P. Gerson, *Hellenistic Philosophy: Introductory Readings* (Indianapolis: Hackett, 1997), pp. 190–260 on Stoic ethics, pp. 139–64 on Stoic theology (or worldview).

For more advanced study, see A. A. Long and D. N. Sedley, *The Hellenistic Philosophers* (Cambridge: Cambridge University Press, 1987). Sections 56–67 are on Stoic ethics; section 54 is on Stoic theology (or worldview). This book gives both translations and commentaries on specific topics. It is referred to as 'LS' throughout this book.

We also list here recent translations of other Stoic writings, including those quoted in this book; translations used are sometimes slightly modified by C. Gill.

Cicero, *On Ends* (Latin, *De Finibus*), Book 3 on Stoic ethics:

Cicero, On Moral Ends, edited and translated by J. Annas and R. Woolf (Cambridge: Cambridge University Press, 2001); this translation is quoted here.

Cicero, *On Duties* or *On Obligations* (Latin, *De Officiis*), in three books.

Translations: *Cicero, On Duties*, edited and translated by M. T. Griffin and E. M. Atkins (Cambridge: Cambridge University Press, 1991); *Cicero, On Obligations*, translated with an introduction and notes by P. G. Walsh (Oxford: Oxford University Press, 2000). The translation quoted here is by Griffin and Atkins.

Cicero, *Tusculan Disputations* (or *Tusculans*). Books 3–4 have extensive discussion of the Stoic theory of emotions, and Book 5 is on ethics and emotions. There is a translation in the Loeb Classical Library series.

Seneca, *Letters* (Latin, *Epistulae*). The translation quoted here is: *Lucius Annaeus Seneca: Letters on Ethics*, translated with an introduction and commentary by M. Graver and A. A. Long (Chicago: Chicago University Press, 2015); there are several other recent translations of selections of letters.

Musonius Rufus, *Lectures*. The translation quoted here is: *Musonius Rufus, That One should Disdain Hardships: the Teachings of a Roman Stoic*, translated by C. Lutz (New Haven: Yale University Press, 2020).

Epictetus, *Discourses* and *Handbook* (*Enchiridion*). The translation quoted here is: *Epictetus, Discourses, Fragments, Handbook*, edited and translated by C. Gill and R. Hard (Oxford: Oxford World's Classics, 2014).

Marcus Aurelius, *Meditations*. The translations quoted here are: *Marcus Aurelius, Meditations*, edited and translated by C. Gill and R. Hard (Oxford, 2011), or *Marcus Aurelius: Meditations, Books 1–6*, translated with introduction and commentary by C. Gill (Oxford: Oxford University Press, 2013).

There are several other recent translations of Epictetus and Marcus Aurelius.

For Stoic theology (worldview) see *Cicero, The Nature of the Gods*, translated with an introduction and notes by P. G. Walsh (Oxford: Oxford World's Classics, 1998).

The works listed here are also all available in the Loeb Classical Library series, Greek or Latin texts with English translations.

DOES HAPPINESS DEPEND ONLY ON VIRTUE?

INTRODUCTION

This exploration of Stoic ethics takes as its starting point the idea that virtue is the only thing that is good and the only basis for happiness. In ancient philosophical debate, this was widely seen as a key distinctive Stoic claim and a controversial one. Different philosophical theories put forward different positions on this question. But an important alternative view, often contrasted in antiquity with the Stoic one, was that of Aristotle and his followers. For this approach, virtue is the most important good thing but things such as health, prosperity and the wellbeing of one's family are also good. Aristotle also maintained that happiness depends on a combination of virtue and these other good things.

The Aristotelian view is often seen as being more plausible and closer to most people's beliefs. Surely, we might think, it is better to be healthy and prosperous rather than ill and poor, and these factors contribute to making us more happy? Why did the Stoics adopt this strong and controversial claim, and why was this topic seen as so important in ancient ethical philosophy?

DOI: 10.4324/9781003499374-2

THE VIRTUE–HAPPINESS RELATIONSHIP IN ANCIENT THOUGHT

When Zeno founded the Stoic school (early third century BCE), the question of the relationship between virtue and happiness was already a central question for ancient ethical theory. It had a comparable importance to questions in modern moral philosophy such as: why should I be just, or why should I act in a way that benefits others, rather than myself, or what counts as a right action and what grounds this idea? Why was the virtue–happiness question so important in ancient thought?

Ancient ethical theory, in general, is centred on agents, their qualities and lives, rather than actions. It is also, typically, focused on the agent's perspective, rather than that of society or some other external standpoint. Virtue and happiness are key ideas in this kind of framework. Happiness (in Greek, *eudaimonia*) is seen as what everyone wants, fundamentally; it is the goal of life, as it is often put. It is also what makes life worthwhile. Thus, ancient 'happiness' is a more substantial idea than it is in modern usage, where it typically refers to a mood or state of mind, sometimes a transient one.

Although this much was common ground for ancient thought, there was room for disagreement about what counted as happiness, both among people in general and among philosophers. In conventional thought, happiness was sometimes identified with pleasure, or a good reputation, or knowledge. It was also often seen as a combination of the things thought to make life worthwhile: health, length of life, prosperity, pleasure, the welfare of one's family and friends, alongside virtue. Philosophers also held divergent views on this question. The Epicureans, contemporaries and rivals of the Stoics, identified happiness with pleasure, understood as freedom from physical pain and mental distress. The previous Greek thinkers who are, in general, closest to the Stoics (Socrates, Plato, Aristotle) stressed the importance of virtue for happiness, though in different ways and degrees.

Virtue (in Greek, *aretē*) is another central idea for ancient ethics; what does this term mean? In Greek thought generally, 'virtue' signifies 'excellence' in some area of life, such as warfare, politics or caring for one's family. For philosophers, the meaning is more precisely defined, though the idea of excellence remains important. Virtue is seen as an excellence bearing on someone's life as a whole, not just in some specific area. It is also a very important quality, indeed, *the* crucial quality, which makes us describe someone as good or bad overall.

For Aristotle, building on the thought of Socrates and Plato, 'virtue' is a good quality of the mind or personality (*psuchē*), rather than the body or an external good thing, such as prosperity. It is also a quality that involves agency or voluntary activity; it is something for which we are at least partly responsible, and for which we can be praised or blamed. The Stoics share Aristotle's view on these points: but they understand this quality as a kind of knowledge or expertise, though one which shapes our character and life as a whole. It is this knowledge that determines whether or not we achieve happiness.

STOICS ON THE VIRTUE-HAPPINESS RELATIONSHIP

It is clear from the points made so far that the ideas of happiness and virtue are central and important ideas in ancient ethical theory. But how are they related to each other? Here too different ancient thinkers hold different views, even thinkers who have a good deal in common in other ways.

Socrates, Plato and Aristotle agree in regarding virtue as the main factor in determining happiness but disagree on one crucial point. Socrates, as presented in Plato's early dialogues, and Plato in the *Republic*, stress the idea that virtue provides the only basis needed for happiness (virtue is both necessary and sufficient for happiness, as it is sometimes put). Aristotle, in his best-known ethical work, the *Nicomachean Ethics* (*NE*), initially seems to adopt the same position (1.7). However, subsequently, he accepts the more conventional view that a happy life also needs other elements too, including length of life, prosperity and a stable family life (*NE* 1.8–10).

The Stoics take a sharply different position from Aristotle, arguing that happiness depends solely on virtue. If someone is virtuous, he or she is therefore happy, regardless of other adversities or losses. As they sometimes put it, the wise (virtuous) person is happy 'on the rack', that is even if being tortured. In antiquity, the Stoics were widely seen as giving the most fully worked-out version of the view that happiness depends solely on virtue.

Why did the Stoics adopt what may seem to be the more extreme position? The Stoic position depends, in part, on their distinction between virtue and 'indifferents' (such as health, prosperity and a stable family life), a distinction examined in Chapter 2. However, their view also depends on their ideas about happiness and virtue, as well as about the virtue–happiness relationship. These ideas, in turn, are supported by reference to their understanding of nature. In this respect, the Stoics see their position as matching human nature, and indeed nature more broadly understood.

We now consider their views more closely. We look at their general statements about the virtue–happiness relationship, and then at their definitions of virtue and happiness. Both virtue and happiness are closely connected with their conceptions of nature; and this connection is crucial for understanding their claim that virtue forms the sole basis needed for happiness.

GENERAL STATEMENTS ON THE VIRTUE–HAPPINESS RELATIONSHIP

The Stoics conceive virtue and happiness as fundamentally linked. This comes out in their definitions of the two concepts and their general statements about the virtue–happiness relationship.

The Stoics conceive happiness as a kind of life, rather than a mood or state of mind. They offer various definitions of happiness (we need to remember that Stoicism is a 'group philosophy', to which different thinkers contribute over time). However, it seems that these definitions are meant to be consistent with each other and, perhaps, aspects of the same idea. For instance, two definitions of happiness attributed to Zeno, founder of Stoicism, are 'consistency' and 'a smooth flow of life'. However, two other Stoic definitions are most important and commonly found: these are happiness as 'the life according to virtue' and 'the life according to nature' (understood as being, essentially, the same thing). So here the link between the two concepts is stated in the strongest possible form: happiness is defined as being the kind of life shaped by virtue.

A similar view comes out in their accounts of virtue. As brought out shortly, virtue is seen as a unified and comprehensive form of expertise. It is sometimes described as 'expertise concerned with the whole of life'. The goal or end of this expertise is to enable human beings to live consistently with nature, which is also to live a happy life.[1] Thus, both happiness and virtue are sometimes defined by reference to each other, and there is a further shared link with nature.

THE STOICS ON VIRTUE

What Stoic ideas about virtue and happiness underlie and support these general statements about the virtue–happiness relationship? Let us take virtue first. As we have already seen, the Stoics, like some other ancient thinkers, see virtue as a kind of excellence, which is a function of the mind or personality and expresses agency and responsibility. It is also a very important, central feature of a person, which determines whether someone is good or bad. How, more precisely, do the Stoics conceive virtue?

Virtue, in ancient and modern ethical thought, is often understood in one of two ways, which may be combined. Virtue can be seen a 'disposition', implying something that is permanent or at least lasting, and is an integral part of the person. This disposition is often seen as involving the whole personality, including emotions or desires as well as rationality. In this sense, virtue 'goes all the way down', as philosophers sometimes say, into the depths of the personality. Virtue in this sense is often associated with the idea of 'character' (in Greek, *ēthos*).

Virtue is also sometimes seen as a kind of knowledge or understanding; or expertise and skill. This kind of knowledge is not localized or specialised; it is knowledge of what is fundamental for living a life. Similarly, the expertise is not localized, but global, bearing on all aspects of living.

Ancient thinkers such as Plato and Aristotle incorporate both these aspects into their conception of virtue. Aristotle, for instance, subdivides virtue into 'character-based virtue' (virtue of *ēthos*) and intellectual or rational virtue, called *phronēsis* in its more practical aspect. The Stoics, typically, define virtue as a form of knowledge or expertise. But this is not meant to exclude the 'character' side of virtue. The Stoics have a highly unified view of the human personality, in which rationality is seen as shaping emotions and desires (see Chapter 6). Hence, virtue as knowledge brings with it the shaping of emotions and desires associated with 'character', as well as the stability associated with 'disposition'.

STOIC VIRTUE: UNITY AND COMPREHENSIVENESS

This combination of features is also coupled with two other characteristics that might seem quite distinct or even opposed to each other. Virtue is seen as highly unified; however, it is also comprehensive, and covers all aspects of a human life. How are these two contrasting features integrated with each other and how do Stoic ideas on this subject relate to their intellectual background?

Aristotle discusses a large number of virtues, both character-based and intellectual ones. Plato's *Republic*, by contrast, focuses on four virtues, seen as core or 'cardinal' virtues: wisdom, courage, temperance or moderation, and justice. He also links them with different psychological functions. The Stoics follow Plato in adopting a framework based on these four cardinal virtues. The four virtues are wisdom (*sophia* or *phronēsis*), courage (*andreia*), temperance, moderation or self-control (*sōphrosunē*), and justice (*dikaiosunē*). However, these are seen by the Stoics as generic virtues or virtue-types, with numerous subdivisions. The four generic virtues correspond to the four main areas of human experience: reasoning and gaining knowledge; responding to danger and challenge; dealing with emotions and desires; forming relationships with other people. The framework is unified in the sense that it forms a single system of virtues; at the same time, the virtue-set covers the whole range of human activity and experience.

There are other ways in which the Stoic virtue-set is unified. This idea is worked out in slightly different ways by different Stoic thinkers. In one version (that of Zeno), all four virtues are seen as modes of wisdom, operating in different sectors of experience. In another version (that of Chrysippus), all four virtues, including wisdom, are seen as expressions of knowledge or expertise, operating in different spheres of activity. The presentation of the virtues as modes of wisdom or knowledge does not mean that they are purely rational or intellectual. On the Stoic unified psychological model, wisdom or knowledge affects someone's whole pattern of emotions and desires, so the virtues shape the personality as a whole.

Another idea associated with Chrysippus is that of the inseparability and interdependence of the four virtues. Each virtue is seen as having a primary area of activity (such as enduring danger or giving people what is due to them), while also, in a secondary way, involving the other virtues and their subject areas. Thus, on any given occasion, the virtuous person is primarily exercising one type of virtue, while also expressing the other virtues in a secondary way.[2]

The theory of the unity or inseparability of the virtues is sometimes criticized as failing to match human experience. Surely, it is argued, different people can have different virtues; for instance, courage can be found in someone who lacks wisdom or justice. However, the Stoics would deny this, for two main reasons. Firstly, each of the virtues are seen as aspects of a single unified type of knowledge or understanding, sometimes presented as knowledge of good and bad and of what should be done on any one occasion. Secondly, each of the virtues is seen as having significant implications for the expression of the other virtues.

The force of this point comes out if we think more closely about courage, for instance. Can we really say that someone has courage if they lack sound judgement (the special domain of wisdom) or if they lack knowledge about giving what is due to other people (the special domain of justice)? Courage without these dimensions would be more like a 'brute' instinct or passion, rather than forming part of virtuous understanding and character. Or can we be expected to show moderation or self-control properly, as regards food and drink or sex, for instance, if we lack sound judgement or an understanding of what is due to other people? If we follow through this line of argument, Stoic ideas about the unity or interdependence of the virtues come to seem more compelling, though they are initially surprising.

In all these ways, the Stoic theory of the virtues combines unity of conception with comprehensiveness of coverage. This explains why the Stoics describe virtue as expertise in the whole of life. But how does this support the Stoic claim that virtue is the only basis needed for happiness? To understand this further claim, we need to examine more closely Stoic thinking about the relationship between virtue and happiness, and the relationship of both concepts to nature.

THE VIRTUE–HAPPINESS RELATIONSHIP

The Stoics stress the closeness of the relationship between virtue and happiness. Indeed, it may seem that they are virtually the same thing. This seems to be suggested, for instance, by this comment: 'Happiness consists in virtue since virtue is a *psuchē* (mind or personality) which has been fashioned to achieve consistency in the whole of life.'[3] But, although these concepts are close in meaning, they are not identical with each other.

For the Stoics, as for other ancient thinkers, virtue is a quality of a person, whereas happiness is a quality of that person's life. Hence, happiness is defined as 'the life according to nature' or 'the life according to virtue'. In this respect, the concept of happiness (a happy life) is broader than that of virtue (a certain kind of understanding and character). Happiness consists of elements which form part of a life lived over time: these include actions and emotions on specific occasions as well as practices and forms of expertise apart from virtue. They also include qualities such as psychological health and beauty, which are characteristic features of a happy life.[4] In this respect, the Stoic concept of happiness is close to the conventional ancient Greek (as well as the conventional modern) view of a happy life as containing several elements which make up wellbeing.

However, the Stoics also stress that what makes these other elements count as 'good', and part of happiness (in their sense) is that they are all uniformly shaped by virtue. These features have no independent goodness; and they are dependent for their goodness, like happiness as a whole, on the person's possession and exercise of virtue. Virtue, we need to remember, is expertise in the whole of life. Thus, although virtue and happiness are differentiated in this respect, the crucial role of virtue as *the* basis for happiness is maintained. This explains the comment quoted earlier. 'Happiness consists in virtue' in the sense that virtue, a quality of someone's personality, pervades the life as a whole and brings about 'consistency', which is one of the marks of happiness.

VIRTUE, HAPPINESS AND NATURE

To understand the way that virtue pervades someone's life as a whole, we need to consider the shared relationship of virtue and happiness to nature. Happiness is often defined as 'the life according to nature'. Virtue is not actually defined as 'knowledge or expertise according to nature'. But virtue and happiness both share the essential features of nature, as the Stoics conceive this.

As brought out in Chapter 3, 'nature' is a complex term, with different senses, in Stoic ethics. However, two senses of 'nature' are especially important: human nature and universal nature (that is, the nature of the whole world or universe). The Stoics highlight what they see as distinctive qualities of human and universal nature. Both virtue and happiness, in different ways, are seen as embodying these distinctive qualities. The fact that *both* virtue *and* happiness embody these qualities is crucial for understanding the relationship between them. It is also crucial for seeing why virtue is the only basis needed for happiness.

HUMAN NATURE

The quality most often presented by the Stoics as distinctive of human beings is rationality. This is understood in terms of functions such as language-use, inferential reasoning, forming judgements and gaining knowledge. Rationality is also seen as informing all other human functions, such as actions, emotions and relationships with other people. A second quality often seen as distinctively human is sociability; the combination 'rational and sociable' is often presented in Stoic sources as characteristically human. All animals are seen as sociable to some extent, for instance, in caring for their own offspring. However, sociability is seen as a more centrally human characteristic and one that is both more complex and potentially deeper, since it is informed by rationality. It is characteristically human to participate fully in family life, friendship and communities; and to recognize that all other human beings form part of a broader community of rational and sociable animals.

In Stoic ethical writings, both virtue and happiness are seen as the highest realization of human nature, conceived as rational and sociable. The four cardinal virtues are seen as the developed expression of four primary inclinations, all of which reflect human nature as rational and sociable. Stoic accounts of ethical development, conceived as 'appropriation', stress both the rational and the sociable dimensions of this process and their integration. The outcome of ethical development is presented as the realization of both virtue and happiness.[5]

Virtue and happiness, as stressed earlier, are expressed in different ways. The virtues are forms of knowledge or expertise, and qualities of a person's personality (*psuchē*), whereas happiness is a form of life, and is a more inclusive concept than virtue. However, virtue and happiness are alike, in Stoic thought, in that they represent the highest realization of human nature (as rational and sociable). Also, both features are linked in that the achievement of happiness depends on one's life being shaped by the expertise of virtue. This point explains why the Stoics define happiness both as 'the life according to nature' and 'the life according to virtue'.[6] This similarity supports the distinctive Stoic claim that happiness depends solely on virtue.

UNIVERSAL NATURE

What is the linkage between virtue, happiness and the natural world as a whole, and how does this support the claim that virtue forms the sole basis needed for happiness?

This is a rather complex question, discussed further in Chapter 3. A key point is that human virtue or happiness and the natural world express the same excellent qualities, though in different but analogous ways. These qualities are structure, order, wholeness and coherence, as well as (in human beings) care for oneself and others of one's kind, paralleling nature's providential care for the universe as a whole.

The idea that virtue and the happiness based on virtue constitute a coherent structure or whole is a recurrent theme in Stoic ethics. This partly reflects the theory of the unity of the virtues and the view that the virtues form a matched set of types of knowledge. It also reflects the Stoic belief that virtue brings with it a consistent pattern of emotions, desires, actions and relationships, whereas vice brings incoherence and internal conflict. Seneca provides a powerful statement of this idea, applied both to virtue and the happiness that derives from the possession of virtue:

> From what, then, did we gain the understanding of virtue? That person's orderliness revealed it to us, his fitting behaviour and consistency, the

harmony among all his actions, and his greatness in surmounting everything. It was thus that we came to understand happiness, the life that flows smoothly and is completely under its own control.

(*Letters* 120.11)

Cicero also describes the virtue and happiness that constitute the outcome of ethical development as constituting 'order and harmony of actions' and as 'consistency' (*On Ends* 3.21).

What is the analogue for this idea in the natural world? The most helpful source for this question is Stoic theology, which forms a kind of 'interface' area between ethics and physics (the philosophy of nature). The Stoics see the universe (and also the world) as forming a coherent and ordered whole, and, in this sense, as expressing a kind of rational structure. A key expression of this is the regular and ordered movements of the sun, moon and planets, which were intensively studied by ancient astronomers. Also, in our world, the cycle of night and day, the tides, the seasons, and the natural processes of birth, reproduction and death are taken as indicators of natural order and coherence.[7]

A second point of contact is this. Nature as a whole (identified with an in-built or 'immanent' god) is seen as the source of energy and vitality. It is also seen as providing the framework which enables all natural entities (including the land, sea and air) to maintain themselves and, in the case of living things, to flourish and, in the case of animals, to reproduce themselves. Nature's role in this respect is sometimes characterized, in anthropocentric terms, as the exercise of beneficence and providential care for the natural world and its contents. One of the indicators of this providential care is the in-built human (and animal) motive to take care of oneself, for instance, the instinct to preserve oneself, and to reproduce and take care of others of one's kind.[8]

As brought out in Chapter 4, these primary motives underpin human ethical development, understood as 'appropriation'. The ultimate outcome of appropriation is the development of virtue and the happiness based on virtue, which are seen as the highest expression of the primary motives to care for oneself and others of one's kind. In this respect, nature's providential care underpins the development of virtue and virtue-based happiness. This helps to explain why Stoic sources sometimes present universal nature or god as the ultimate basis of human virtue and happiness.[9]

Thus, overall, the Stoics see virtue and the happiness based on virtue as expressing the qualities of human nature at its best and also those of the natural world. The linkage between virtue, happiness and nature consolidates other points of connection between virtue and happiness, and supports the distinctive Stoic claim that virtue is the sole basis needed for happiness.

MODERN APPLICATIONS

Most of us come to the study of ethics with pre-existing ideas about happiness. We talk about happiness all the time in daily life, but we may have never thought seriously about it before. Pause for a moment and think about the last time you told someone you were happy. What exactly did you mean by 'happy'? What led you to feel this way? How long did your happiness last?

If you're following conventional usage, your 'happiness' was probably a transitory emotion which was based on external conditions. We tend to say we're 'happy' when we go on holiday, or the weather is nice, or we get an extra scoop of ice cream with double chocolate chips. But ancient Greek thinkers would not label this short-lived emotional response *happiness*. For them, happiness (*eudaimonia*) results from striving to live a meaningful and flourishing life. They would say that happiness is not a fleeting emotion but a lasting way of life based on our understanding and character – based on virtue, as they put it. Some systems of virtue ethics (such as Aristotelianism) suggest that happiness depends both on an internal factor (virtue) and external factors. But the Stoics were exceptional in insisting that *eudaimonia* depends solely on the quality of our understanding and character, not on the external conditions of our life. We do not become happier by acquiring more wealth, fame or power. We become happier by pursuing virtue.

Why would this be so? It all goes back to our key defining characteristics as humans: rationality and sociability. Excellence in these areas is what we call virtue. Because this represents the best of human nature, you might say that virtue is the completion or perfection of our nature. The ancient Stoics believed all humans have the starting points of virtue; we are all capable of developing in this direction. One ancient source tells us that Cleanthes (331–232 BCE), the second head of the Greek Stoa, compared humans to 'half-lines of iambic verse; if they remain incomplete they are base [foolish], but if they are completed they are virtuous'.[10] In a metaphorical sense, we are all unfinished lines of poetry striving to find fulfilment by completing our nature.

We can easily test out some of these ideas for ourselves. Let's think for a moment about *fulfilment*, which shares some characteristics with *eudaimonia*: it usually occurs over a period of time, rather than as the product of momentary pleasure; it results from meaningful actions that connect you to a broader purpose; it reflects your values; it results from your own agency, not random events or other people's actions. Think back to the times in your life when you've felt most fulfilled. What were you doing, and why were you doing it? How would you describe your mental attitude or condition while experiencing fulfilment? Does it contribute to personal and moral growth and to your involvement in relationships with others and your community? Is this a condition worth pursuing in life? While fulfilment is only a partial approximation of *eudaimonia*, thinking about it can help us start to understand how *eudaimonia* might structure our lives in a different way from conventional ideas about happiness.

Once we stop thinking about happiness as a transitory feeling and start thinking about it as a long-lasting psychological condition, we can see why it is so closely linked to virtue in Stoic ethics. If we see happiness as dependent on external conditions, we are likely to pursue those conditions above all else. If, however, we see happiness as a deep, long-lasting internal state that results from the fulfilment of our human nature, i.e. virtue, we take a completely different approach to life and to ethics.

Let's consider two examples of how these differing conceptions of happiness might influence our behaviour towards other people.

EXAMPLE 1: A BIG MISTAKE

You are backing your car out of a parking spot one day when you accidentally back into another car, leaving a small dent in it. Oops! Fortunately, no one is around to see you. You could easily drive away with no outward repercussions for yourself. (You try not to picture the other driver returning to discover that their car has been damaged and they will be forced to pay for repairs.) If you are primarily focused on happiness as a feeling of pleasure or enjoyment – and lack of external negative consequences – you might be tempted to choose this option. It's certainly the easiest, cheapest and least embarrassing for you.

On the other hand, you might have a nagging feeling that decision wouldn't be right. If the situation were reversed, and someone else dented your car, you would definitely want them to pay for the damage. You wonder if you should stop and leave a note on the other car's windscreen with your name and phone number, offering to pay for repairs. Clearly, this is both inconvenient and costs you money, but deep down you know this is the right thing to do.

What do you decide to do? What considerations go into your choice?

If you are a Stoic and you see happiness as determined by virtue, you will be much better off doing what you think is right, no matter how inconvenient it is. You know that if you drive away without leaving a note, you will have dented your character as well as the car. Not only have you let someone else down, ruining their day and making the world a slightly less trustworthy place, you have let yourself down too. You'll carry the inner shame of having behaved badly, which is not conducive to living a truly happy or flourishing life.

If you decide to leave a note offering to pay for the damage, you will suffer some inconveniences in the short term, but you will emerge from the situation with your character intact. Accidents happen and everyone makes mistakes sometimes, but your response to those accidents and mistakes creates your character. If you habitually respond to challenging situations by prioritizing excellence and virtue, you create the basis for an authentic and meaningful happiness. As Marcus Aurelius (*Meditations*, 3.12) reminds us:

> If you hold to this, awaiting nothing and fleeing from nothing, but remaining satisfied if your present action is in accordance with nature, and if all that you say and utter accords with the truthfulness of an earlier and purer age, you will live a happy life; and no one can stand in your way.

EXAMPLE 2: CAREER

What do Stoic concepts of virtue and happiness have to do with the big-picture questions of life, such as choosing and conducting a career? Since we spend the bulk of our waking hours engaged in work activities, we want to make sure our career aligns with our ethical principles.

If our ethics emphasizes pleasure (Epicureanism) or virtue mixed with worldly 'goods' (Aristotelianism), we might give more weight to the external rewards of a career: making lots of money, enjoying social prestige, winning awards and recognition, getting promotions. But in Stoic terms, these external rewards are 'preferred indifferents' (discussed further in Chapter 2). They are nice to have, but not the primary determinants of our happiness in life. The primary determinant of happiness is virtue, knowing that our work is contributing to excellence of character for ourselves and a better world for other people.

In practice, this means we pursue a career that allows us to maintain an exemplary character. The good news is that there are many jobs that qualify. You can help others and stay true to your principles as a lawyer or accountant, a teacher or social worker, a plumber or delivery driver. These all provide necessary services and can be done in a way that truly brings benefit to others. All these career choices can align with virtue and result in a flourishing life. (On the other hand, all of these could also be done badly, resulting in unhappiness on all sides.)

What about a career with specifically ethical aims, such as working for a non-profit company or charity that helps children or the environment? Again, these jobs can be done well or badly. The non-profit world is full of wonderful people tirelessly improving society and the planet, but there are also some people selfishly pursuing their own aims through a thinly veiled guise of helping others. It's not uncommon for well-meaning altruists to become discouraged and burn out from these careers due to the disappointing realities of money, politics and hypocrisy.

The point is: there are many fulfilling career options for people of good character. While you may decide to pursue a career in a helping profession or a position where you can effect social change, there is ample scope for virtue and happiness in a variety of jobs. (For example, don't you want both your doctor and your electrician to be honest and competent?) No job is perfect, and we will inevitably have to deal with difficulties and challenges no matter what career we pursue. But the Stoics counsel us to find work well-suited to our particular personality and abilities, where we can make a contribution to the world and enjoy sharing our gifts with others.

NOTES

1 IG: 126–8; LS 63 A.
2 IG: 127; LS 61 D.
3 LS 61 A.
4 LS 60 J–M.
5 IG: 125–6; Cicero, *On Duties* 1.11–15. On 'appropriation' and ethical development, see Chapter 4.
6 IG: 132–3; LS 63 A.
7 Cicero, *The Nature of the Gods* 2.15, 43, 54–6, 97 (IG: 61, 67–8).
8 Cicero, *The Nature of the Gods* 2.57–8, 73–153, especially 126–8 (IG: 68, 69–77, especially 74).
9 Cicero, *On Ends* 3.17, 20–1, 62–8 (IG: 152–3, 156–7); LS 57 A, F, 59 D. Also LS 60 A, 63 C.
10 IG: 128.

FURTHER READING

B. Inwood, *Stoicism: A Very Short Introduction* (Oxford: Oxford University Press, 2018), 65–78.

J. Sellars, *Stoicism* (Chesham: Acumen, 2006), 122–9.

For more advanced study:

J. Annas, *The Morality of Happiness* (Oxford: Oxford University Press, 1993), chs. 2 and 19.

C. Gill, *Learning to Live Naturally: Stoic Ethics and its Modern Significance* (Oxford: Oxford University Press, 2022), ch. 1.

K. M. Vogt, 'The Stoics on Virtue and Happiness', in C. Bobonich (ed.), *The Cambridge Companion to Ancient Ethics* (Cambridge: Cambridge University Press, 2017), 183–99.

Ancient writings on virtue and happiness:

Cicero, *On Ends* 3.20–50.

IG: 124–33, 151–7.

LS, sections 60, 61, 63 (good, virtue, happiness); also 54 (on theology/worldview).

Modern applications of the Stoic theory:

M. Pigliucci, *How to Be a Stoic: Ancient Wisdom for Modern Living* (London: Penguin, 2017), ch. 7.

D. Robertson, *Stoicism and the Art of Happiness* (London: Hodder & Stoughton, 2013), chs. 2–3.

K. Whiting and L. Konstantakis, *Being Better* (Novato: New World Library, 2021), chs. 1–2.

HOW DOES VIRTUE RELATE TO OTHER VALUES?

INTRODUCTION

The Stoic claim that virtue is the sole basis for happiness depends partly on the idea of virtue as expertise in living a happy life and on the linkage between virtue, happiness and nature. But it also depends on the idea that there is a radical distinction in value between virtue and other things that are often valued. As the Stoics put it: virtue and virtue-based happiness are the only good things, whereas other things often seen as good are only 'indifferents'. The point is not that these other things are unimportant; they are 'indifferent' because they do not meet the criterion of being good, and they do not *make the difference* between happiness and misery, as the Stoics understand these notions.

In ancient philosophy, the Stoic position was often contrasted with that of Aristotle and his followers. According to Aristotle, although virtue is the most important factor, happiness also requires at least a minimum level of bodily and external goods; that is, things such as health, possessions, and the wellbeing of family and friends. Aristotle's key example is Priam, who, by the end of the Trojan War, had lost all his wealth, power as king of Troy and most of his large family (*NE* 1.8–10). No one, Aristotle says, could call someone in that situation happy. The Stoics, however, would argue that if Priam was, indeed, virtuous, as Aristotle assumes, he was for that reason also happy, despite his great losses. In a famous image, they assert that the wise (virtuous) person is happy 'on the rack'; that is, even if he is being tortured.

This chapter explores Stoic thinking on virtue and indifferents by considering a series of questions. What exactly is the basis for the Stoic distinction between virtue and indifferents and does it explain their view that virtue, but not indifferents, count as good? What are the respective roles of virtue and indifferents in a good human life and how are they interconnected? What contribution is made to Stoic ethics by introducing the idea of indifferents? Is the Stoic idea of indifferents defensible against the criticisms of it made by ancient or modern thinkers?

At this point, we need to note a partial disagreement on this subject among different Stoics. The mainstream Stoic view, that of two heads of the Stoic school, Zeno and Chrysippus, is that indifferents can be subdivided between 'preferred' and 'dispreferred'; that is, things which do or do not have positive value. For instance, health and prosperity are 'preferred' or 'preferable', whereas illness and poverty are 'dispreferred' or 'dispreferable'. However, one early Stoic, Aristo, rejected this distinction, arguing that the only significant point is the difference between virtue and indifferents. Indeed, he maintained that virtue consists in recognizing the fact that all indifferents are ethically non-significant.[1]

This more radical version of the Stoic theory seems to have influenced Epictetus and Marcus Aurelius, who make little reference to the idea of preferred and dispreferred indifferents. However, the mainstream view is the dominant one in the main sources for Stoic ethics and is the version mostly discussed here.

THE DISTINCTION BETWEEN VIRTUE AND INDIFFERENTS

The key Stoic claim is that virtue is good, whereas indifferents are neither good nor bad. Virtues such as wisdom, courage, temperance and justice are good whereas things such as health, prosperity and the welfare of our families are neither good nor bad, even though they are things that human beings naturally want to have and so are, in Stoic terms, 'preferable' rather than 'dispreferable'. What is the basis of this claim? To make sense of this, it is useful to refer to the way that the Stoics analyse goodness. Although the Stoics do not offer formal definitions of goodness, two ideas are dominant in their discussions. One is the idea of benefit. What is good benefits us consistently and by its nature. A second idea is that goodness is constituted by the perfection of our human nature; that is, our nature as rational animals. On the Stoic view, rationality is a quality shared by human beings at their best and the universe as a whole. Hence, goodness is the perfection of our rational nature as human beings, which is also in line with universal nature.[2] These two criteria may seem unrelated but they can be connected in various ways. For instance, to achieve the perfection of our nature is to gain the greatest possible benefit. As we will see shortly, this is how the Stoics understand virtue, as distinct from the preferred indifferents.

How do the Stoics support the claim that things such as wealth and health, while naturally 'preferred', are not good? There are two main lines of argument. One is that, whereas virtue benefits us consistently and by its nature, things such as wealth or health, poverty or illness neither benefit nor harm us. A second argument is that what can be used both well and badly is not good. But it is possible to use wealth and health both well and badly, and so they do not count as good. The second argument helps to clarify the first. Since wealth, for instance, can be used well or badly, it cannot be said to benefit or harm us consistently and by its nature; in this sense, it neither benefits nor harms us.[3]

What exactly do the Stoics have in mind in arguments of this kind? At a certain level, the point is a rather straightforward one. For instance, someone could inherit great wealth, and this new acquisition might upset or undermine her existing pattern of relationships with family and friends. Thus, she would gain one preferred indifferent (wealth), but lose another (a stable pattern of relationships with family and friends). Or someone might be called up for military service because he was healthy and end up dying in battle. Thus, it becomes clear that things such as health and wealth do not benefit us consistently and by their nature. In cases of this kind, the benefit is only at the level of preferred indifferents; someone gains one preferred indifferent and thereby loses another. However, the Stoics mainly have in view a deeper understanding of benefit and harm.

To make sense of their view, we need to examine more closely how they conceive the difference between preferred indifferents and virtue. First of all, what kind of things count as indifferents? Here is one ancient list: 'for instance, life, health, pleasure, strength, wealth, reputation, noble birth and their opposites, death, disease, pain, ugliness, weakness, poverty, low repute, ignoble birth and the like'. From this list, you might think that preferred indifferents correspond to what Aristotle, for instance, describes as bodily goods, such as health, and external goods, such as a flourishing family. By contrast, for Aristotle, mental goods include things such as intelligence or virtue. However, the Stoics sometimes include among preferred indifferents mental qualities such as 'natural ability, (ethical) progress, good memory'.[4] So, there is more to the distinction than that between mental and physical or external qualities. What else is involved?

The Stoic Epictetus sometimes contrasts 'externals' (his term for indifferents) with 'choice' or 'decision' (*prohairesis*) and with what is 'up to us' or 'within our power'. For Aristotle too, virtue is a mental quality that involves voluntary action, deliberation and choice; it is also a quality in line with practical reason, ensuring that the choice is correct.[5] The Stoics have a rather different psychological framework from Aristotle (discussed in Chapter 6); but their understanding of virtue is similar in this respect. Virtue is not just a mental quality, such as natural intelligence or good memory (which are preferred indifferents). Virtue also involves agency, voluntary action and decision. Also, virtue enables us to make decisions correctly and at the deepest level. Hence, virtue is characterized by the Stoics as a form of knowledge or expertise, namely expertise in living a happy life; that is, a life according to nature.

Thus, the difference between preferred indifferents and virtue is this. The preferred indifferents, such as health, wealth or good memory, are things that can, in principle, make a positive contribution to our lives and which we naturally want to have. But they are not the central structuring factors in our lives, which make the difference between a life well lived and one that is lived badly. The virtues, by contrast, are central expressions of our agency, and shape the nature and quality of our motivation, actions, emotions and relationships with other people. They are also crucial forms of knowledge or expertise, determining whether we live well or badly; they also determine whether we do or do not lead a happy human life, that is, a life according to nature.

This distinction helps to explain why the Stoics maintain that virtue benefits us (consistently and by its nature), whereas the preferred indifferents do not; the indifferents do not have this central, structuring role in determining whether we live a happy life. The virtues enable us to select or reject things such as health, wealth and reputation, in a way that enables us to live a good human life. As the Stoics put it, the virtues enable us to make 'right use' of indifferents, both preferred and dispreferred.[6] The virtues, as forms of knowledge and expertise in living a life according to nature, also constitute the perfection of our rational nature.

So, once explained, the Stoic distinction between virtue (as good) and indifferents (neither good nor bad) makes good sense, despite the rather unfamiliar terminology and claims. Indeed, it offers an illuminating insight into the question of what is involved in leading a good life. At the same time, it challenges the conventional assumption that what determines our happiness or misery is the presence or absence of things such as health, wealth and reputation.

THE RELATIONSHIP BETWEEN VIRTUE AND INDIFFERENTS

If only virtue (and anything that depends on virtue) is good, does this mean that a good human life is one lived without any indifferents at all? This makes no sense. Indifferents form the material of a human life and are crucial for motivation. Virtue without indifferents would be, in the image of *Alice in Wonderland*, like the smile of a Cheshire cat when the cat has disappeared. Nor can there be a happy human life without any preferable indifferents. Even the wise person happy on the rack of torture has one preferred indifferent, namely life. So the question is this: what is the proper relationship between virtue and indifferents in a good human life?

For the early Stoic thinker, Aristo, whose approach differs from most Stoics on this point, virtue consists in being indifferent to indifferents.[7] The virtuous person takes no account of the difference between health or illness, wealth or poverty; her virtue consists in being indifferent to such things. This view is challenged by mainstream Stoic thinkers, such as Chrysippus, the third head of the school. They argue that, on Aristo's view, wisdom or virtue would have no function, and there would be no basis for the distinctions that are essential for living a normal human life.[8]

Chrysippus also asked: 'What should I take as the basis for appropriate action and the material of virtue, if I pass over nature and what is in line with nature?'; that is, preferred indifferents, such as health and wealth.[9] It is significant that preferred indifferents are also called 'things according to nature', meaning that they are things it is natural for human beings to pursue. This does not mean that simply acquiring such things enables us to live 'the life according to nature'; that is, happiness. However, it does indicate that acquiring 'things according to nature' can, in principle, contribute towards happiness.

Indeed, Stoic thinkers regarded distinguishing between preferable things such as health or wealth and their opposites as an integral part of the good (virtuous and happy) life. Several heads of the Stoic school after Chrysippus defined happiness or the goal of life in terms of the selection of preferable things. We are told that the wise person reasonably decides to end her life if her only prospect is a life of pain; that is, if the balance between preferable and dispreferable indifferents points only towards dispreferable ones. The wise or virtuous person also understands the significance of the difference between preferable and dispreferable indifferents. She does so even after coming to recognize that virtue and not the preferable indifferents count as really good.[10]

What is suggested by these points is that *part* of the expertise of virtue lies in correct understanding of the value of indifferents, both positive and negative, for living a good human life. This makes good sense. How can someone be brave, for instance, if she has no understanding of the significance of danger and risk to life? Such a person would be just a hurtling automaton, rather than brave. How can someone be generous (generosity forms part of the cardinal virtue of justice) if she lacks a proper understanding of the positive value of gifts of money, status or other benefits for those to whom she aims to be generous? This point comes out very clearly in Cicero's *On Duties* Book 1. In offering guidance on the kind of actions that are in line with the virtues, Cicero refers extensively to the correct calculation of the positive and negative value of preferred and dispreferred indifferents (see also Chapter 5).

However, this does not mean that the virtuous person's expertise consists *only* in correct estimation of the positive or negative value of indifferents. Virtue, as we have seen, constitutes 'right use' of indifferents. It is not enough just to add up the positive and negative value of the indifferents that form part of one's life. Virtue may also require us to give up a preferred indifferent or accept a dispreferred one with a view to leading a virtuous life. 'Right use' of indifferents means using them in a way that can enable someone to live a life 'according to nature'. This means, in part, using them in a way that is consistent with exercising the virtues (all four virtues, as a matched set). It also means using indifferents in a way that enables us to lead a life according to the best qualities of human and universal nature, in the sense discussed in Chapter 1. This is a life marked by the best possible combination of rationality and sociability, and also by order and coherence, and proper care for ourselves and others of our kind.

This explains why the Stoics say that virtue benefits us whereas indifferents neither benefit nor harm us. Virtue benefits us by providing the best possible benefit, namely that of living the best possible human life, and one that is also in line with universal nature. Virtue brings about the perfection of our nature (by reference to human and universal nature) and thus makes our lives good. Gaining preferable indifferents does not produce this kind of benefit, nor does losing them harm us in the way that loss of virtue does.

Whether or not making right use of indifferents means acquiring preferred indifferents or giving them up depends on the circumstances of our life at any one time. In some situations, acting according to the virtues may coincide with gaining preferred indifferents for ourselves or others, though this should not form the primary basis for our decisions. In other situations, the brave or generous-minded action may involve giving up all preferred indifferents, including life. However, the Stoics believe that in all situations, the virtuous person can make a decision that enables her to live a happy life, a life 'according to nature', and in this sense virtue always confers benefit.

IS THE IDEA OF 'INDIFFERENTS' A GOOD ONE?

The term 'indifferents' is unfamiliar. But does the idea make an important contribution to Stoic ethics and can it be defended against the criticisms directed at it in ancient philosophical debate?

It certainly contributes significantly to Stoic ethics, not least by helping to explain why Stoics maintain that virtue and things dependent on virtue constitute the only good and that virtue is the only basis needed for happiness. Also, we see in later chapters that the virtue–indifferents distinction is crucial for other important features of Stoic thinking. It plays a major role in their thinking on ethical development, practical deliberation, emotions, and social and political relationships.

However, the idea was attacked by other ancient thinkers and its value has sometimes been questioned by modern scholars. Can these criticisms be answered? One criticism was that the Stoic theory introduces two overall goals in life (virtue and preferred indifferents). Yet the Stoics, like other ancient ethical approaches, maintained there was only one overall goal.

However, this criticism can be met. The Stoics recognize only one overall aim, happiness conceived as the life according to virtue or according to nature. Achieving this goal normally involves pursuing preferred indifferents. But the aim is not just to gain things such as health and wealth but to do so *in a certain way*, and certainly not at all costs. The Stoic aim is to gain them in a way that is consistent with acting virtuously and with bringing about the life that matches the best standards of human and universal nature. Hence, the Stoic theory is consistent in this respect.

Another criticism was that the Stoic idea of preferred indifferents is, essentially, just the same as the more familiar Aristotelian idea of bodily and external goods, and that it adds nothing further to understanding ethical life. However, this criticism too can be answered. The two ideas differ especially on one very important point. Aristotle thinks that, if someone suffers a really serious loss of bodily and external goods, his happiness is inevitably affected, even if he is virtuous. As noted earlier, he cites the example of Priam who lost his kingdom and most of his family; and he argues that no one could call Priam completely happy even if he continues to be virtuous.[11] However, for the Stoics, if Priam is indeed virtuous, he is, by that fact alone, happy in their sense; he is still living the life according to human and universal nature. What he has lost are preferred indifferents, not things that are good, and in this respect he has not lost his happiness.

Ancient thinkers following the Aristotelian approach regard the Stoic position as incredible on this point and as failing to recognize the realities of human nature and experience. However, the Stoics address this criticism too. They cite cases where people choose to act bravely or in a generous-minded way, even when this involves them in serious losses. Their examples include famous Roman heroes such as Regulus, who chooses to return to certain torture and death for the sake of his nation and in commitment to his oath. The Stoics also point out that ordinary, less morally exceptional, people regularly endure pain, hardship or even death for things they see as really important.[12]

Someone such as Regulus acts virtuously, even at the loss of things that human beings naturally want to have; that is, preferred indifferents. In Stoic terms, he is still happy, in the sense that he is meeting the highest standards of human and universal nature. The Stoics also regard such people as happy in a further sense and one that is closer to the modern conception of happiness as an emotion or state of mind. Such people approach their difficult or dangerous situations with single-minded commitment and whole-hearted acceptance of the loss that is involved. In Stoic terms, they confront their situation without 'passions', which are marked by intensity and internal conflict, and with 'good emotions' such as wish and joy, an idea discussed in Chapter 6.

The Stoic view has a credibility we can recognize today. On a daily basis, we expect members of our society to risk their lives for a worthwhile cause within their personal or professional life. They may be members of the armed services, firemen or medical staff working in dangerous conditions, or parents rescuing their children from danger. Despite the potential or actual losses involved, we too can see these people and their lives as good and, in some sense, happy. We too find it credible that those acting in this way do so with single-minded commitment and accept the consequences with calm resignation and without emotional conflict. In taking this view, we are adopting a picture of human nature similar to the Stoic one. We accept that it falls within recognizable human experience to act virtuously even at the loss of things we would normally want to have (preferred indifferents) and to accept this consequence emotionally.

The Stoics recognize that the question what does or does not fall within the scope of human nature and capacities is a complex one. This comes out in their discussions of the idea of nature in general, and of ethical development, which they see as a natural process, including emotional development. However, from the points made in this chapter, it is clear that the Stoics can make a strong response to the criticism that their account of the relationship between virtue, happiness and indifferents fails to match the reality of human nature.

MODERN APPLICATIONS

At first sight, the Stoic doctrine of indifferents might seem counterintuitive, even paradoxical. How could conventional goods such as health, wealth and social status not contribute to our happiness? However, as demonstrated above, the Stoics had very convincing reasons for assigning a different value to virtue and indifferents. We'll consider three examples of what this distinction might look like in everyday life.

EXAMPLE 1

Let's say you have what would be considered a conventionally happy life: good health, a good job, good relationships and financial security. Now let's say you face some sort of dilemma that might threaten one of these 'goods'. Perhaps you realize the company you work for has been stealing from its customers. If you report the criminal actions of your company, you know you will face repercussions such as losing your job, and you may not be able to get another one. This would impact on your financial security and perhaps even your health and relationships. Would you choose to jeopardize your job, financial security, health and relationships in order to 'do the right thing'? How would you weigh the concrete risks to your personal situation against the abstract virtue of protecting unknown customers?

From an Aristotelian perspective, you would probably render your life unhappy if you chose to report your company's actions against your own interests. Without the job, you would lose several of those things that you think contribute to your happiness. What incentive is there to do the right thing if you lose all chance of being happy?

From a Stoic perspective, however, the choice is clear. By doing the right thing you benefit both society and yourself. How do you benefit yourself? Because all those conventional goods, job, health, relationships, financial security, are indifferents, and they are not required for a good and happy life. What *is* required for a good and happy life is virtue. If you lose your job, you still have the possibility of happiness. But if you harm your own character and ethical understanding, you lose the possibility of true happiness.

EXAMPLE 2

Now consider a person who is born into poverty in a war-torn nation. Conventional morality might suggest that such a person has no chance at happiness; their life will be bleak and miserable unless their material condition improves.

Stoicism rejects this hopeless conclusion. It is possible for such a person to experience character-based happiness, despite their poverty and the instability of their community. Indeed, in these difficult conditions virtues often shine forth all the more brilliantly, as evidenced by historical accounts from many bleak episodes in world history. This is what we mean by saying earlier that 'virtue involves agency, voluntary action, and decisions'. The external conditions of our lives provide the context for us to exercise our agency through virtue. We can respond to the same material conditions in a virtuous or a non-virtuous way, thereby creating happiness or unhappiness for ourselves.

It is important to note, however, that even though Stoics do not think anyone is a prisoner of their material conditions, we should still do our utmost to help other people, animals and the environment. As already noted in this chapter, Stoics do see a type of value in the 'things according to nature' such as health, financial security and a well-functioning society. It is reasonable for people to pursue these indifferents in a way compatible with virtue. We work towards these things for ourselves and others while at the same time recognizing that we all have the capacity for happiness even if these conditions are not present in our lives. This will be discussed in more detail in later chapters, especially Chapter 5 on practical decision-making.

EXAMPLE 3

On the opposite end of the spectrum, consider the example of someone who has great wealth and privilege but who is still unhappy. We are familiar with many examples of celebrities and other wealthy people who, despite literally having everything they could want, continue to chase after more things, never satisfied. You might even have experienced some version of this for yourself. Have you ever worked hard to get something – a new phone, a holiday, a promotion – only to feel let down after you got it? As Seneca reminds us, if such things could really satisfy us, they would have already:

> Dismiss at last those treacherous goods that are more valuable in expectation than they are in attainment. If there were anything solid in them, we would eventually be sated with them; as it is, they make us thirsty even as we drink.
>
> (*Letters* 15.11)

Reflect for a moment on your life and the lives of everyone you know. If material things could really make us happy, then the last shiny new phone you got would have set you up for the rest of your life. But that's not what happened, is it? All the material things we've ever had haven't produced long-lasting happiness for us (or anyone else). So happiness must lie elsewhere, not in the things themselves.

NOTES

1 LS 58 E–G.
2 LS 60 G–H.
3 IG: 117–18; LS 58 A.
4 IG: 117–18, 134.
5 Epictetus, *Discourses* 1.1; Aristotle, *NE* 2.6, 3.1–3.
6 IG: 117–18; LS 58 A.
7 LS 58 G.
8 Cicero, *On Ends* 3.50.
9 LS 59 A.
10 IG: 132; LS 58 K; Cicero, *On Ends* 3.21–2, 3.60–1 (IG: 153).
11 Aristotle, *NE* 1.10.
12 Cicero, *On Duties* 3.99–115 (Regulus); on Regulus, see also Chapter 5, pp. 80–81. Cicero, *Tusculans* 5.76–9 (brave acts by ordinary people).

FURTHER READING

B. Inwood, *Stoicism: A Very Short Introduction* (Oxford: Oxford University Press, 2018), 78–87.

J. Sellars, *Stoicism* (Chesham: Acumen, 2006), 110–14.

For more advanced study:

C. Gill, *Learning to Live Naturally: Stoic Ethics and its Modern Significance* (Oxford: Oxford University Press, 2022), ch. 2, 54–72.

B. Inwood, and P. Donini, 'Stoic Ethics', in K. Algra, J. Barnes, J. Mansfeld and M. Schofield (eds), *The Cambridge History of Hellenistic Philosophy* (Cambridge: Cambridge University Press, 1999), 675–738, especially 690–7.

Ancient Stoic writings:

IG: 117–18, 133–6.

LS sections 58 (indifferents), 60 (good), 64 (ancient debate on Stoic ethics).

Modern applications of the Stoic theory:

D. Fideler, *Breakfast with Seneca: A Stoic Guide to the Art of Living* (London: Norton, 2022), chs. 6, 8.

W. A. Irvine, *A Guide to the Good Life: The Ancient Art of Stoic Joy* (Oxford: Oxford University Press, 2008), chs. 14–15.

N. Sherman, *Stoic Wisdom: Ancient Lessons for Modern Resilience* (Oxford: Oxford University Press, 2021), ch. 3.

IS STOIC ETHICS GROUNDED ON NATURE?

INTRODUCTION

The topic of nature differs from most of the other chapter-topics in this book. Other chapters treat subjects which form standard items in the three main ancient summaries of Stoic ethics. 'Nature' is not a standard topic of this kind. However, the phrase 'according to nature' and the ideas of human or universal nature are pervasive in Stoic ethics. It is understandable, then, that modern scholars have raised questions about the role of nature in Stoic ethics. In the absence of authoritative Stoic texts explaining this role, in a sustained, analytic way, it is not surprising that scholars have reached different conclusions about this subject.

One view that is often put forward is that universal or cosmic nature is not just an important idea in Stoic ethics but is basic or *foundational* for the whole ethical framework. This view is common both among modern scholars and those who adopt Stoicism as a way of life. The core ideas and principles of Stoic ethics, about virtue, happiness and indifferents, are seen as being *dependent,* in a strong sense, on universal or cosmic nature. This view is based on certain ancient passages, considered later, as well as on certain well-marked links between the Stoic worldview and ethics.

However, other scholars question the idea that cosmic nature is foundational for ethics. It is striking that, in the three ancient summaries which form our main primary evidence for Stoic ethics, the theories of virtue, happiness and indifferents are sometimes presented in their own terms, or are linked with human nature, rather than cosmic nature. There are also no sustained formal arguments in the ethical summaries, or elsewhere, explaining how the claims about the virtue–happiness or virtue–indifferents relation are derived from the Stoic worldview or god. If cosmic nature was, indeed, foundational for Stoic ethics, this idea would surely have been more consistently emphasized and more systematically worked out than it is. Certainly, cosmic nature is important for the Stoics; but this does not mean that it forms the foundation for ethical theory. This alternative view is the one adopted here.

The question of how to interpret the role of nature in Stoic ethics is pursued further later in this chapter. To provide a basis for considering this question, we begin by reviewing the full range of ways in which the concept of nature is presented in ancient Stoic ethical writings. The main evidence considered here, as elsewhere in this book, is the three ancient summaries of ethics, taken with some related material.[1]

We can identify three principal ways in which the idea of nature appears: as human nature; as human nature considered alongside animal nature and in a broader natural context; and as cosmic or universal nature. To provide a wider framework of reference, we begin by considering a way of presenting Stoic ethics in which the idea of nature does *not* appear, or at least does not play a major role. This is, in fact, the most common way of presenting Stoic ethical concepts in the summaries; in this sense, ideas about nature supplement or enhance the standard presentation of ethics.

FOUR TYPES OF PRESENTATION OF STOIC ETHICS

TYPE (1): ETHICAL CONCEPTS

In all three ancient ethical summaries, key concepts and claims are often stated, and argued for, with little or no reference to the idea of nature. This applies to the distinctive Stoic claims already discussed about virtue as the only good and as the only basis needed for happiness, and about the distinction between virtue and indifferents. The goodness of virtue is explained in terms of types of knowledge or expertise, which justifies the claim that virtue enables 'right use' of indifferents and thus benefits the virtuous person. In all three summaries, it is argued that what is good (virtue) is also beneficial because it is useful, and worthy of being praised and chosen. These claims about the goodness of virtue also underpin the subsequent accounts of the role of virtue in deliberation and action, in emotions, and in interpersonal and social relationships (examined in Chapters 5–7). These further ideas are also, for the most part, framed in purely ethical terms.

Type (1) presentation is the dominant mode of exposition and argument in the summaries. Thus, it is clearly regarded as a way of expressing ethical ideas that is valid in its own right. However, it would be misleading to say that type (1) presentation makes *no* reference to nature. In all three summaries of Stoic ethics, we find the ideas that indifferents are 'according to' or 'contrary to' nature, and that happiness or the goal of life is 'according to nature'. These terms occur even when there is no attempt to spell further what kind of nature (human or universal) is involved. In this sense, type (1) presentation is interwoven with the language of nature even though the predominant form of expression in the ethical summaries is in terms of types of value.

TYPE (2): HUMAN NATURE

The second type of presentation combines ethical ideas expressed in terms of type (1) with reference to distinctively human nature, typically defined as rational and sociable. This is a rather frequent feature of Stoic ethical writings. It is particularly prominent in one of the three main ancient summaries of Stoic ethics, where it forms a key theme in the analysis of the concepts of virtue and happiness and of their relationship.[2]

In this summary, virtue is presented as a form of knowledge which is characteristic of human beings, conceived as distinctively rational and sociable. The four cardinal virtues are described as based on four primary inclinations, which chart the four main areas of human experience.

These inclinations are: 'to discover what is appropriate, to stabilize one's motives, to stand firm, and to distribute fairly'; these underlie the four cardinal virtues of wisdom, moderation, courage and justice.[3]

Also, happiness (conceived as the life according to nature) is associated specifically with human nature, as rational and sociable; and virtue and happiness are associated with each other in this respect. This paves the way for the conclusion that happiness is both the life according to virtue and the life according to nature, here meaning according to human nature.

> Since a human being is a rational, mortal animal, sociable by nature ... all human virtue and happiness constitute a life which is consistent and in agreement with nature ... that is why the Stoic goal [the life in agreement with nature] is equivalent to the life according to virtue.[4]

The underlying line of thought is this. Both virtue and happiness express the distinctive qualities of human beings at their best, a combination of rationality and sociability. This, in turn, supports the Stoic definition of happiness as both a life in accordance with virtue and a life in accordance with nature (meaning here, human nature). It also supports the Stoic claim that virtue, and not the preferred indifferents, provides the sole basis needed for happiness. Virtue does so because it expresses the best possible qualities of human nature, which are also crucial for happiness.

We find a similar set of ideas in another Stoic ethical work, Cicero's *On Duties*. Book 1 begins by presenting the idea of human beings as, characteristically, rational and sociable. The four cardinal virtues are then presented as rooted in four primary human inclinations, which express this combination of rationality and sociability. Again, these primary human inclinations are for rational understanding, for managing emotions and desires, responding to danger and challenge, and forming relationships with other people; and these inclinations underpin the virtues of wisdom, moderation, courage, and justice (1.11–15).

The overall presentation of the virtues in *On Duties* Book 1 also brings out the idea that the virtues constitute the realization of human nature as rational and sociable. Each of the four cardinal virtues is presented in a two-fold way, first as a form of (rational) expertise in living, and then as an expression of the motive to benefit others. Courage is described first as the ability to withstand dangers and adversity and then as readiness to undertake socially beneficial activities which involve risk. Justice is defined first as proper treatment of other people and property and then as active engagement in human association. A further strand of justice is beneficence or generosity, directed at helping others for their own sake. Temperance or moderation combines thoughtful management of emotions and desires with respectful and considerate treatment of others. Wisdom is defined first as the discovery of truth, and, in a later discussion, as reason directed at social benefit.[5] This two-fold analysis of the virtues and their underlying motivation reflects the Stoic conception of human beings as, characteristically, both rational and sociable, and as naturally disposed to care for others as well as themselves.

Also, at various points throughout the work, Cicero brings in the idea of human nature to support his exposition. He refers especially to the idea that different forms of community, such as family or nation, derive from our fundamental human rationality and sociability and the bond that this creates between all human beings, the 'brotherhood of humankind'.[6] As these writings bring out, the linkage between virtue and human nature forms a significant strand in Stoic ethical thinking.

TYPE (3): CONTEXTUALIZED NATURE

This mode of ethical presentation is similar to type (2) in being centred on the distinctive capacities and qualities of human beings. However, there are two further aspects.

One is that human motivation is seen as a more advanced (rational) version of types of motivation shared with other animals. Human beings and other animals are seen as motivated by two basic, in-built, instincts, to care for themselves and to care for others of their kind (in the first instance, their offspring).

Secondly, the presence of these motives is presented as an expression of a broader natural pattern. The fact that animals have these basic motives is taken to expresses the providential care of cosmic nature (or god) for all elements in the natural world, including animals and human beings. The fact that animals naturally seek to preserve their lives and wellbeing and that of their young is taken as an expression of nature's providential care. These ideas are brought out in Stoic writings on ethical development conceived as 'appropriation' and on theology or the worldview.[7]

In human beings, these primary motives form the basis for ethical development, which is sometimes presented as taking two main forms. The basic motive of care for oneself forms the starting point for the development of virtue and virtue-based happiness, which constitute the fullest realization of human natural capacities. A key feature of this strand of development is the progressive understanding of the proper value of virtue and indifferents, considered in relation to each other. In the second strand of ethical development, involvement in family, community and political relationships is presented as a developed version of the basic in-built motive of care for others. By implication at least, these more advanced human functions are presented as expressing nature's providential care for human beings as distinctively rational animals.[8] In these respects, type (3) presentation extends the sense of 'nature' involved to include universal or cosmic nature as well as human nature.

TYPE (4): COSMIC NATURE AS AN ETHICAL IDEAL

What about 'nature' in the sense of the natural world or universe, cosmic or universal nature? The natural world appears as part of a larger set of ideas in type (3) presentation, for instance, in connection with the view of development as appropriation; but sometimes it appears on its own in ethical writings. In fact, in the three ancient summaries of ethics, there is rather little discussion of cosmic nature (which forms the central topic of Stoic theology); but there are two important passages, which also match evidence from other sources.

One passage, at the end of Cicero's account of Stoic ethics in *On Ends* 3, refers to the relationship between the study of universal nature and ethics, as types of intellectual enquiry:

> The starting point for anyone who is to live in accordance with nature is the universe as a whole and its government. Also, one cannot make correct judgements about good and evil unless one understands the whole system of nature and indeed the life of gods, as well as the question whether human nature matches universal nature.
>
> (3.73)

This idea is confirmed by comments of Chrysippus quoted in other authors; here is one such comment:

> it is not possible to find another starting point (*archē*) or another origin for justice other than the one from Zeus and from universal nature; it is from this that every such thing must have its starting point, if we are to say anything about goods and evils.[9]

Another important passage is also attributed to Chrysippus:

> Therefore the goal becomes 'to live consistently with nature' i.e. according to one's own [human] nature and that of the universe, doing nothing which is forbidden by the common law, which is right reason, penetrating all things, being the same as Zeus, who is the leader of the administration of things. And this itself is the virtue of the happy person and a smooth flow of life, whenever all things are done according to the harmony of the *daimōn* [guardian spirit] in each of us with the will of the administrator of the universe [i.e. Zeus].[10]

This passage is quite compressed as well as complex in its meaning. But the main point is that there is a close link between god or Zeus, the shaping force (or 'administrator') of the universe, and the mind (or 'guardian spirit') of the virtuous human being. Virtue and virtue-based happiness are presented as constituting 'harmony' between the will of Zeus and the mind of the virtuous human being.

Thus, virtue and virtue-based happiness consist in 'the life according to nature' in the sense of a life that is in line both with human nature at its best and with cosmic or universal nature. One clear link between these three ideas (virtue, human nature and cosmic nature) is rationality or 'right reason'. Human nature, as we have seen, is characterized as rational (and sociable). In this passage, cosmic nature is also associated with 'right reason', and both of these types of nature form a basis for virtue, which Stoics conceive as knowledge or expertise, notably expertise in leading a happy life; that is, a life according to nature.

It is also likely that this passage presupposes two other connections between virtue or happiness and god, conceived as the animating force and organizer of the natural universe. One linkage consists in the ideas of structure, order and wholeness, or, overall, consistency. These are notable characteristics both of the natural universe and of virtue and happiness, as conceived by the Stoics. Another salient theme in Stoic theology is the idea of divine providential care for all aspects of the natural world. This theme is connected especially with Stoic thinking about appropriation: the in-built motives of care for oneself and others are seen as an expression of this broader providential care. Although these links are not explicit in the passage, they may be implied in the idea of a 'harmony' between Zeus as organizer of the natural universe and virtue or happiness.

SCHOLARLY DEBATE

It is obvious, from this review, that there is rather wide variation in the way that nature is presented in Stoic ethics, even within the three ancient summaries of ethics. What overall view can we form about its role and significance?

As stated at the start, a common view is that Stoic ethics is grounded on universal or cosmic nature or god. This view is based primarily on the evidence of presentation type (4). However, a problem for this view is that Stoic ethics is not consistently presented in this way in our main sources. Nor is there any systematic explanation of how, exactly, cosmic nature explains and justifies the core principles of Stoic ethics. The distinctive Stoic ideas about virtue as the sole basis for happiness, and about the virtue–indifferents contrast, are, typically, stated and argued for on different grounds, in presentation type (1). The linkage between nature and these key ethical ideas is most fully spelled out in presentation type (2), where they are connected with human nature, rather than cosmic. Further connections are made between ethical principles and human or universal nature in presentation types (3) and (4).

Taking all this into account, we can form an alternative view of the role of nature in Stoic ethics to the idea that this is grounded on cosmic nature. This alternative view differs in three ways from the foundational view: 1) This view gives weight to the fact that the core ideas of Stoic ethics (about virtue, happiness and indifferents) are often stated, and argued for, in their own terms, and seem to be treated as valid by themselves. 2) Hence, references to nature are seen as supporting or enhancing ethical principles rather than grounding them or providing foundations. 3) It is not only cosmic nature that provides this support; it is also provided by human nature and comparison between the nature of human beings and other animals.

This alternative interpretation is the one adopted here, though it should be noted that the view that Stoic ethics is grounded on cosmic nature or god is the more common one both among Stoic scholars and people using Stoicism as a source of life-guidance.[11]

THE ANCIENT CONTEXT

What is the broader context of ancient thinking on nature, god and ethics? Is there any one view on this subject that was regarded as standard or orthodox?

In ancient Greek culture, it was not generally assumed that ethical principles were grounded on beliefs about the gods or about the natural world. There is a strong contrast in this respect with the traditional view in Western culture that Judaeo-Christian religion and its worldview provide the ultimate grounding for morality. There was also widespread debate in Greek philosophy about the relationship between nature, the gods and ethics. The Epicureans, contemporaries and rivals of the Stoics, argued that there was no connection between the nature of the world or universe and human ethics.

However, in thinkers whose ideas are generally close to Stoicism, we find connections made between ethics and the ideas of human or cosmic nature. For instance, in Plato's *Republic*, it is argued that justice, as analysed there, corresponds to key features of human nature and psychology. Also, Aristotle uses the idea of human nature as a way of defining and supporting his conception of happiness as virtuous activity (*NE* 1.7). So in these cases, the linkage stressed is between ethics and human nature.

On the other hand, there are parallels between the worldview presented in Plato's *Timaeus* and Stoic theology. Both theories present the universe as shaped by god, in different ways, and as embodying ethical principles. According to both theories the universe is ordered and coherent; it is also organized by god's providential or benevolent care, which is built into the natural order. Both theories also sometimes suggest that the order of the natural world offers an ethical model for human beings.

Overall, reference to earlier Greek ideas helps to provide a broader context for the Stoic use of the idea of nature in ethics. However, the background is quite complex; and comparison with earlier ideas does not resolve the question how to interpret the role of nature in Stoic ethics.

THE MODERN CONTEXT

Can reference to modern thought on this question help to provide parallels for the Stoic approach? Perhaps surprisingly, there is a suggestive parallel.

The range of possible modern positions on the role of nature in ethics is extremely wide. Many of these approaches have little in common with Stoicism (on either of the interpretations discussed here); however, one is close to the Stoic approach, as interpreted here. A notable feature of current moral philosophy is the revival of theory centred on the ideas of virtue and happiness, generally called 'virtue ethics'. This represents an alternative to more standard forms of modern moral theory, focused on ideas of duty or human benefit (see Chapter 8).

An important strand of modern virtue ethics is based on Aristotelian ethics, and this approach has a good deal in common with Stoic ethics. Certain thinkers in this strand follow Aristotle and Stoicism in incorporating ideas of nature into their ethical framework. These thinkers are Elizabeth Anscombe, Philippa Foot and Rosalind Hursthouse. A shared idea is that the virtues are those qualities that enable someone to lead a good human life; and a good human life is one that expresses the capacities and qualities characteristic of human beings. Hence, moral goodness is not seen as an abstract or 'non-natural' quality (as maintained by some modern philosophers); it corresponds to the highest expression or flourishing of human beings.

Should we suppose that this approach is designed to replace the normal ethical standpoint with a 'scientific' one, based on study of human nature? No. The aim is, rather, to enhance or supplement the ethical standpoint with an understanding of the way in which the virtues enable one to lead a good human life. The aim is not to replace 'values' with 'facts', but to show how reference to the facts of human life enables us to make sense of our ethical values. Acting virtuously is still seen as intrinsically good, and not simply instrumental to some other end. However, the naturalistic approach helps us to understand the basis for this goodness.

This modern approach is close to the Stoic use of the idea of nature in ethics, as interpreted here. In the terms used earlier, this approach combines presentation type (1) with types (2) and (3). These modern thinkers adopt ideas about virtue and happiness which are comparable in kind with those found in presentation type (1). However, they also enhance or supplement these ideas by connecting them with an understanding of human nature, conceived as distinctively rational and sociable (type (2) presentation), and by correlating human nature with that of other animals (an aspect of type (3) presentation).

However, there is no equivalent in modern naturalistic virtue ethics for the idea that nature as a whole is inherently ordered and forms an ethical model for human beings; or for the idea of nature as a whole as benevolent or as exercising providential care (that is, ideas linked with presentation type (4) and, to some extent, type (3)). To this extent, the parallel between the Stoic and modern theories is not exact. However, in other respects, the similarities are striking and illuminating.

CONCLUSIONS

In this chapter, we have considered what is perhaps the most complex and difficult aspect of Stoic ethics, and the one that has generated most scholarly debate in recent years. The main evidence for this question has been set out and analysed, in terms of the four types of presentation of Stoic ethics. Two interpretations have been outlined: the idea that Stoic ethics is grounded on universal or cosmic nature, and an alternative view, in which ideas of nature enhance or supplement ethical ideas which are also seen as valid in their own terms. The Stoic theory has been placed in a broader context within ancient thought, and compared with one modern approach, that of naturalistic virtue ethics.

MODERN APPLICATIONS

Ethics is a complex subject, and there are many ways of thinking about, and arguing for, different ethical positions. As explained here, in the ancient summaries of Stoic ethics we find four primary types of presentation. Three of the four are based in 'nature', in various senses, while the first and most common type relies more on ethical reasoning of a kind that is often found in Greek philosophy. Scholars will probably continue to debate the relative importance of each of these types in ancient Stoicism. What's important for applied ethics, however, is how this variety of approaches can be useful for us today. We'll summarize the four types again briefly and then think about how they can help us in ethical deliberation.

TYPE 1: ETHICAL CONCEPTS

What general concepts, definitions and principles can we use to organize our thinking on ethics? In Type 1 reasoning, ethical concepts and propositions are connected by analysing the relationship between them. This type of analysis may refer to nature (for instance, in the phrase 'according to nature') but does not depend on a specific idea of nature for its conclusions.

The ancient Stoics often explained their ethical positions through definitions, for instance defining 'the good' as 'that from which there is something beneficial'. After proposing this definition, the Stoics examined how it could be applied to many different things we label 'good', including people, actions, the results of actions or non-human entities. One benefit of this type of analysis is that we can move between abstract theory and concrete applications, applying theoretical concepts to a wide range of practical situations.

TYPE 2: HUMAN NATURE

Does the fact that we are human mean we think and act differently than if we were spiders, hedgehogs or some form of extraterrestrial life? Of course! It sounds like a silly question, but the fact that the answer is so obvious just underscores how important our nature is – so important that we sometimes take it for granted or forget about it. The kind of creature we happen to be makes a big difference in our capabilities, instincts and behaviour. For example, it may be perfectly appropriate for a polar bear father to abandon his cubs or a black widow spider to kill her mate, but these actions would be wrong for a human being. As Seneca reminds us:

> How will you know what conduct should be adopted unless you have discovered what is best for a human being and have studied human nature? You will not understand what you should do and what you should avoid until you have learned what you owe to your own nature.
>
> (Seneca, *Letters*, 121.3)

Since human beings are naturally rational and social creatures, we are good when we behave in a way that matches this nature. Our ancestors successfully survived and passed down their genes by cooperating and forming cohesive groups, and these groups in turn cared for each individual member. This is still the way human beings flourish today, and our ethical systems are based on, and promote, rational and social behaviour.

TYPE 3: CONTEXTUALIZED NATURE

Where do humans fit into the bigger picture of the natural world? Although the ancient Stoics thought humans were superior to other forms of life, they also recognized that every creature, from dogs to bulls to bees to humans, flourishes when it fulfils its purpose. As the Roman Stoic Musonius Rufus explained, 'The nature of each [creature] guides it to its own excellence' (*Lecture* 17). In some ways, then, humans are no different from other animals, plants or even the universe as a holistic system. This contextualized perspective will be extremely important for an updated Stoic environmental ethics (which we will look at in Chapter 9).

TYPE 4: COSMIC NATURE

In what way does our understanding of the cosmos influence our ethics? The ancient Stoics thought of the cosmos as a single living entity and as a model of rational and orderly activity. Because nature is reliably structured and functions as an internally coherent system, they thought humans should act in the same way.

Some ancient Stoics, particularly Epictetus and Marcus Aurelius, felt we should strive to be rational and benevolent in the same way that the universe as a whole is rational and benevolent. This was sometimes expressed in theological terms, as when Epictetus says, 'In place of all other pleasures, introduce that of being conscious that you're obeying God' (3.24.110).

Sometimes it was reflected in a recognition that humans are just one small part of the cosmic whole:

> Always keep the following points in mind: what the nature of the whole is, and what my own nature is; and how my nature is related to that of the whole, and what kind of a part it is of what kind of a whole, and that no one can prevent you, in all that you do and say, from always being in accord with that nature of which you are a part.
>
> (Marcus Aurelius, *Meditations* 2.9)

APPLYING THE FOUR TYPES TO CONTEMPORARY ETHICS

As you can see from this passage of Marcus Aurelius, the various types of ethical presentations were frequently used together. It is significant that Stoic ethics references all four, and all four can be used in various ways to support Stoic principles. This variety can be a source of philosophical strength. Based on your own experience, do you see an advantage in approaching ethics from multiple angles? Which of the four types of presentation do you think are the strongest or work best together?

Approaching ethical questions from different angles can help to generate new insights into complex issues and ethical dilemmas. For example, when thinking about bioethics, we might focus on arguments from the perspective of Type 2 (human nature) and Type 3 (contextualized nature). When considering our response to climate change, we might find special value in Types 2 (human nature), 3 (contextualized nature) and 4 (cosmic nature). When looking at political systems, we could focus on Types 1 (ethical concepts) and 2 (human nature).

You might also think about how each of these types can help with practical ethical questions in your own life. Perhaps you find one or more of these types of presentation especially useful when dealing with grief, or thinking about death, or deciding what job to take, or what to eat for dinner. In general, the better our tools and resources for examining ethical issues, the more clarity we gain in our ethical choices. In this way, the four types of presentation of Stoic ethics offer a useful framework for our moral thinking today.

NOTES

1 For these summaries and their importance as evidence for Stoic ethics, see Introduction, p. 00, and the Further Reading for that chapter.
2 The summary of Stobaeus, generally seen as based on the thought of the major Stoic theorist Chrysippus, mediated through Arius Didymus (late 1st century BCE).
3 IG: 125–6.
4 IG: 132–3.
5 Cicero, *On Duties* 1.18–19, 20–2, 42, 66, 93, 99–104, 153–4.
6 Cicero, *On Duties* 1.50–9, 3.21–7, 3.52–3.
7 IG: 113, 156–7; LS 57 A, F; Cicero, *On Ends* 3.62; Cicero, *The Nature of the Gods* 2.126–9 (IG: 74).
8 On these two strands of ethical development, conceived as 'appropriation', see Cicero, *On Ends* 3.16–22, 62–8, as well as Chapter 4.
9 LS 60 A.
10 IG: 114; LS 63 C(3–4).
11 For examples of different scholarly approaches, see Further Reading.

FURTHER READING

For an overview of this topic, see J. Sellars, *Stoicism* (Chesham: Acumen, 2006), 125–9, also 91–5, 99–104, 107–9.

For competing views on the question of the role of nature in Stoic ethics, see A. A. Long, *Stoic Studies* (Cambridge: Cambridge University Press, 1996), chs. 6, 8, presenting Stoic ethics as grounded on cosmic nature, and J. Annas, *The Morality of Happiness* (Oxford: Oxford University Press, 1993), ch. 5, challenging this view and stressing the role of ethical concepts, taken on their own, and human nature.

See also C. Gill, *Learning to Live Naturally: Stoic Ethics and its Modern Significance* (Oxford: Oxford University Press, 2022), ch. 3, reviewing the whole question, and ch. 7 (especially 279–92) on modern naturalistic virtue ethics and Stoicism.

Modern naturalistic virtue ethics:

E. Anscombe, 'Modern Moral Philosophy', *Philosophy* 33 (1958), 1–19.

P. Foot, *Natural Goodness* (Oxford: Oxford University Press, 2001).

R. Hursthouse, *On Virtue Ethics* (Oxford: Oxford University Press, 1999), chs. 8–11.

HOW DO WE LEARN TO BE GOOD?

INTRODUCTION

Ethical development (or learning how to become a good person) is a major theme in Stoicism, as in ancient philosophy generally. This reflects the ancient focus on agents, and their virtue or happiness, rather than right actions, which has been the main topic in modern philosophy, at least until recently. In ancient thought, study of ethical development served, in part, as a way of exploring what virtue and happiness consisted in and how they were expressed. Since ethical development is so central for ancient thought, it is a subject on which Greek and Roman philosophy is well placed to contribute positively to modern theory.

This chapter begins by outlining the general characteristics of Stoic thinking about ethical development, by contrast with some other ancient approaches. We then focus on their most important and distinctive theory in this area, that of development as 'appropriation' (*oikeiōsis*). The following two chapters (Chapters 5–6) also discuss ethical development in connection with deliberation about actions and with emotional responses. Stoic thinking on ethical development is thus highly inclusive, embracing these three areas of human experience, as well as being highly integrated. It is also closely linked with the ideas on virtue, happiness, indifferents and nature treated in earlier chapters. The internal coherence of Stoic ethics is a well-marked feature of their theory and is one we aim to bring out in this book.

DISTINCTIVE FEATURES OF STOIC THINKING ON DEVELOPMENT

The special characteristics of the Stoic approach come out most strongly if we contrast them with a pattern of thinking we find in Plato, especially the *Republic* and *Laws*, and Aristotle, in the ethical works and *Politics*. In the Platonic–Aristotelian pattern, there are two main, interconnected, features. Ethical development is seen as based on a combination of inborn nature (*phusis*), habituation (*ethos*) in beliefs, attitudes and emotions (especially in childhood and youth), followed by intellectual or rational education (*logos*). Also, ethical development is subdivided between two phases, one largely habituative and directed at training emotions and attitudes, and the second more rational or theoretical, aimed at producing ethical understanding or knowledge. This pattern is worked out in these Platonic and Aristotelian writings in terms of educational frameworks set in political contexts.

The Stoic pattern of thinking differs in several respects. The distinctive Stoic features consist in emphasis on universality and naturalness, combined with a focus on adult life and ongoing aspiration.

The Platonic–Aristotelian pattern assumes that different people are very unequally placed as regards their scope for ethical development. Whether or not they develop the virtues and achieve happiness depends on a special combination of internal and external factors. These factors include having a natural goodness of character and an inborn capacity for intellectual education and also having the suitable social or political context for proper upbringing and advanced education.

The Stoics, by contrast, stress that, as Cleanthes puts it, 'all human beings have the starting points of virtue'.[1] These starting points consist, partly, in what the Stoics call 'preconceptions' (*prolēpseis*); that is, the inborn capacity to form a conception of key ethical ideas such as 'good'. They also consist in the in-built basic motives, to care for yourself and for others, that all human beings have and which form the basis for ethical development understood as 'appropriation'. In this respect, the Stoics have a more universalist approach to ethical development, as they do in their social and political thinking more generally.

A further aspect of their universalist approach is this. The Stoics believe that ethical development can occur in any social or political context, and that the capacity to develop ethically forms part of the natural human make-up. Thus, in their accounts of appropriation or guidance on practical decision-making, they present ethical development as taking place in and through activities that form part of any typical human life.

The Stoics recognize, like Plato and Aristotle, that family and social contexts can provide both positive and negative influences on development. However, they think that human beings have the in-built capacity to discriminate between positive and negative influences and thus gradually build up a better understanding of virtue and happiness.

Linked with the universalist approach is the idea that ethical development, taken as a whole, is a natural process for human beings, rather than one that depends on a combination of (a special kind of) inborn nature, habituative upbringing, and intellectual education. The sense in which this development is 'natural' is quite complex, as brought out especially in connection with appropriation. But a key point is that appropriation, like other aspects of ethical development, is seen as expressing our nature as human beings and enabling us to live the best possible form of life for human beings.

Plato and Aristotle conceive ethical development as a two-stage process, in which habituation during childhood and youth provides the foundation needed for rational ethical education in adult life. The Stoics, on the other hand, present ethical development as a single, continuous process of learning. This process presupposes rational development, to some degree at least; hence, the Stoics focus on adult life, when human beings are thought to acquire rationality. However, the Stoics locate the start of adult rationality quite early, at fourteen or even seven, in certain respects. The Stoics see ethical development as a process in which the person is actively engaged, developing her critical faculty and understanding, not just passively accepting social influences or an intellectual framework; and this active role is primarily a feature of adult life.

Although the Stoics present complete ethical development as something that all human beings can, in principle, carry out, they also stress that completing this process is a rare and difficult achievement. The one who does so is the ideal 'wise person', the model of ethical perfection. Hence, for virtually all of us, ethical life is, at best, a matter of ongoing 'progress' towards virtue and virtue-based happiness. Although progress falls short of perfection, making progress is seen as inherently worthwhile and as a process that matches our human nature and capacities.

APPROPRIATION (*OIKEIŌSIS*): THREE-FOLD PATTERN

The characteristic Stoic approach to ethical development underlies various aspects of their thinking. A very important aspect is their theory that human development, including ethical development, can be interpreted as a form of 'appropriation' (*oikeiōsis*). The Greek term suggests making something 'one's own' (*oikeios*). There is no obvious English equivalent; scholars use 'familiarization', 'endearment' or 'orientation', as well as 'appropriation'.

In accounts of this theory, we find a three-fold pattern, though not all accounts contain all aspects of the pattern: 1) The Stoics highlight widespread patterns of human behaviour, which are shared, at a basic level at least, with other animals. 2) These patterns of behaviour are explained, in the first instance, by certain motives or instincts, shared by humans and other animals, namely self-preservation and the desire to procreate and care for one's offspring. These basic motives are analysed, in turn, as the expression of two core dispositions: to care for oneself (or one's make-up or 'constitution'), and to care for others of one's kind. 3) It is maintained that these dispositions form an in-built element in human (and animal) nature, and that they express nature's providential care for all aspects of the natural world. As it is sometimes put, (universal) nature 'appropriates' us (cares for us) and this leads us to 'appropriate' ourselves and others of our kind by caring for them.

This three-fold pattern explains the starting point of ethical development (in human beings); it also underpins the later stages, though in a more complex way. Let us look more closely at the basic motives, and then consider how far the pattern also explains advanced stages of ethical development.

BASIC MOTIVES

There are clear examples of the three-fold pattern in connection with both care for yourself and for others. The natural instinct for self-preservation, in all animals, including human beings, is taken as evidence of a broader underlying disposition, to care for oneself or one's constitution (one's physical and psychological make-up). This disposition is conceived as being to 'appropriate' oneself; and this disposition is seen, in turn, as an indication that nature as a whole 'appropriates' the animal or makes it 'its own'.[2]

A similar pattern is evident in the case of care of others. The primary evidence of this disposition is the fact that animals, including human beings, are instinctively driven to procreate and care for their young. The fact that animals are naturally equipped for procreation, by their bodily shape, from birth to some extent, along with the widespread instinct to care for one's young, is taken as showing that universal nature exercises providential care for animal reproduction. The motive to care for one's offspring, like the instinct for self-preservation, is seen as indicating a broader underlying disposition, to care for others of one's kind. In Stoic theology, universal nature is presented as exercising providential and benevolent care for all aspects of the natural world. One aspect of this providential care is the fact that animals are naturally equipped and motivated to maintain their own lives and to reproduce themselves and care for their young.[3]

Although some accounts present each of these basic motives separately, they are sometimes coupled with each other. A comment preserved by Plutarch, an ancient critic of Stoicism, shows that this combination of the two basic motives goes back to the early Stoic thinker Chrysippus:

> Why then, in heaven's sake, in every work on physics and ethics does [Chrysippus] weary us to death in writing that we are appropriated (*oikeioumetha*) to ourselves, as soon as we are born, and to our parts [our bodies], and our offspring?[4]

It is worth noting that the Stoics, in this respect, see care for ourselves and for others as equally basic or core motives for human beings and, indeed, other animals. Hence, ethical motivation is not seen by them, as sometimes in modern thought, as consisting in the modification or transformation of an instinctive self-centredness into care for others. Both basic motives are regarded as part of our in-built nature; the disposition to care for others is not seen as one that depends purely on social training. Both basic motives need ethical development for their full expression; this applies to the motive of care for others as much as the motive of care of oneself.

ETHICAL DEVELOPMENT: FIRST AND SECOND STAGES

What is the process by which the basic motives are developed ethically, that is, by which human beings acquire virtue and virtue-based happiness?

The fullest account is given as part of Cicero's summary of Stoic ethics in *On Ends* 3. Here, the discussion is subdivided into the development of care for ourselves and of care for others. However, it is clear from Cicero's account and from other evidence, that ethical development involves the combination and integration of both kinds of care. The expressions of both kinds of care are combined and interlinked in lived human experience. There are significant connections between the development of both kinds of care, which, taken together, express our human nature as both rational and sociable.[5]

In Cicero's account, the development of self-care in human life is broken down into three main stages. The first stage is that in which the activities expressing the basic motive of self-care are informed by rationality. The Stoics see rationality as a distinctively human capacity, not shared with other animals, that develops during the transition from childhood to adulthood. The rational functions of adult human beings include language-use, logical reasoning, forming judgements, exercising critical appraisal, and seeking and gaining knowledge. The Stoics see rationality as shaping all other psychological functions, including the formation of motives and actions.[6]

Animals and human children instinctively exercise self-care by avoiding risk to life and injury or painful situations. In adult human life, this develops into a more general pattern of seeking 'things according to nature' (or 'preferable indifferents') and avoiding their opposites. People seek things that promote life, health, prosperity, a stable family life, and so on, and avoid their opposites. In adult human beings, this process involves the exercise of rational functions; Stoics characterize this process as 'selection' of 'things according to nature'.

In the case of self-care, this process consists of seeking and gaining such things for oneself. However, in normal experience, where both kinds of care are combined, it also involves 'selecting' such things for other people with whom one is concerned, most immediately one's own family. So the development of care for oneself and others goes through parallel stages and is interconnected.[7]

This point helps us to make sense of the second stage in the account of ethical development in Cicero, *On Ends* 3.20. This stage links selection of preferable things with the performance of 'appropriate actions' (*kathēkonta*). Like indifferents, this is a technical term in Stoic ethics (explained in Chapter 5). Put briefly, these are the actions that human beings normally perform and regard as appropriate. These actions, like indifferents, may be either self-related or other-related. They include, for instance, taking care of your health (self-care) and respecting your relatives and country, or spending time with friends (care of others).[8] Thus, 'selecting indifferents' and performing 'appropriate actions' are two, interconnected ways, in which human beings develop ethically, using their rational capacities both in caring for themselves and others.

This combination of activities is presented as the means by which human beings develop an understanding of virtue or what is really good. The transitional process leading to this understanding is not described in much detail in *On Ends* 3.20. Cicero only says that the selection carried out is increasingly 'consistent' and 'in full accordance with nature', phrases that are regularly associated with Stoic ideas about virtue and virtue-based happiness. Cicero's main aim is to show how the process of developing towards virtue forms a natural extension of the activities linked with the primary motives of self-care and, implicitly, care of others.

However, the process of developing an understanding of what the virtues involved is discussed much more fully in *On Duties* Book 1. This discussion also explores more fully the interconnections between performing 'appropriate actions' and 'selecting indifferents' in a way that promotes an understanding of what it means to act according to virtue (see Chapter 5).

ETHICAL DEVELOPMENT: THE THIRD STAGE

The third and final stage in Cicero's developmental sequence is described more fully; and this clearly represents both the climax of ethical development and the main point of the whole account. Crucial for this stage is a certain kind of recognition or understanding, though this carries with it a profound transformation of motivation and objectives.[9]

What is recognized or understood is what really counts as good, namely virtue and virtue-based happiness. Cicero's phraseology for the good, including 'right actions and the right itself', 'regularity and order of actions', and 'consistency' (*homologia*), can cover both virtue and happiness. The good is characterized by comparison with preferred indifferents (or things according to nature). The developing person recognizes that the good (virtue and happiness) is the only proper standard of action and the only thing that is intrinsically desirable and the proper object of choice. Hence, motivation is directed solely towards acting and feeling in line with the good.

This recognition carries with it a new valuation of things such as health and wealth (preferable indifferents), which constitute the main object of concern in the previous stages. The developing person recognizes that these things are not intrinsically valuable and desirable. However, the understanding achieved is not wholly negative in its valuation of preferables. First, selection of indifferents, along with performance of appropriate actions, forms the route by which an understanding of the proper value of virtue is achieved. Second, selection between indifferents continues to be the means by which virtue is expressed. This selection needs to incorporate an awareness of the difference in value between preferred and dispreferred indifferents. Although this distinction is less significant than that between virtue and indifferents, it is one that still plays a valid role in virtuous decision-making.

Thus, Cicero's account of ethical development charts a movement from primary self-care (the basic motive) to an understanding of the most important ideas of Stoic ethics. Those who have completed this process recognize that virtue, along with virtue-based happiness, is the only thing that is intrinsically good, and also, by implication at least, that virtue is the sole basis needed for happiness. This final phase also incorporates the mainstream Stoic view that preferred indifferents have positive value, but not goodness, and that virtuous selection needs to take account of the difference between preferred and dispreferred differents.

CARE FOR OTHERS OF OUR KIND

Cicero's account of the development of self-care in his summary of Stoic ethics in *On Ends* 3 (3.16–22) is the most important single ancient source for our knowledge of this topic. Similarly, his discussion of the proper expression of care for others in *On Ends* 3 (3.62–8) is a very important source for the social dimension of ethical development.[10] Although Cicero does not restate the three-stage developmental sequence in connection with the expression of care for others, there are significant parallels between the two strands in development. Also, as pointed out already, complete ethical development involves the combination and integration of both kinds of care.

The Stoics regard the universal instinct of self-preservation as the primary indicator that care of self is an in-built human motive or disposition. Similarly, the primary indicator of care for others is the universal human instinct, shared with other animals, to procreate and care for one's offspring. The presence of this natural instinct, along with that of the reproductive organs in our bodily make-up, is seen as showing nature's providential care for human and animal regeneration. In these respects, care for others, like care for oneself, is seen as having a well-marked basis in human nature (and, to some extent, universal nature).

In the three-stage developmental sequence just outlined, the basic motive (for self-care) is enhanced by rationality, thus providing the basis for ethical development in human beings. This is expressed especially in performing 'appropriate actions' and 'selecting between indifferents'. Analogously, in social development, features such as involvement in family and community life, and other-benefiting actions such as making a will, are seen by Stoics as advanced, rational expressions of the primary motive of care for others. Another aspect of the social strand in development is coming to understand that all human beings, as rational and social animals, form a single broad community or family.[11]

The final stage of the developmental sequence set out in the case of self-care consists in understanding that virtue constitutes what is really good and the sole basis needed for happiness. Analogously, Cicero's account of the development of care for others culminates in the expression of virtues, such as justice or generosity, in actions that benefit others. These actions are associated with the ideal wise person or symbolic figures representing the wise person. Cicero highlights the labours of the hero Heracles, performed on behalf of humanity as a whole, and also the willingness of the wise person to engage fully in family and political life.[12] Thus, Cicero's discussion shows how care for others, as well as care for oneself, can form the underlying motive for all three stages of ethical development, as the Stoics conceive these.

These parallels between the expression of self-care and care for others brings out two further significant features of Stoic thinking on ethical development. The first, as already noted, is that, in lived human experience, ethical development involves the expression of both kinds of care, in combination and in an interconnected form. This is the case, although in Cicero's summary of Stoic ethics in *On Ends* 3, Cicero discusses the two forms of care separately. The other point is that caring for others, on its own, is not inherently good; we can go wrong in this area just as much as in caring for ourselves. Both in-built human motives, care of self and care of others, need the developmental process that leads towards virtue before they are expressed properly.

CONCLUSIONS

What are the main features of the Stoic theory of appropriation, and how far do they reflect the general characteristics of their thinking on ethical development, by contrast with that of other ancient theories?

As noted earlier, in Plato and Aristotle, we find a rather different pattern of thinking, in which complete ethical development depends on a combination of a special kind of inborn nature, social habituation and intellectual education. The stress on the importance of instilling the right kind of attitudes and emotions in childhood and youth is also one that has been taken up by some modern theories of ethical development.

The Stoic theory of appropriation differs from these accounts in emphasizing that ethical development is a natural process. This point applies to the basic motives from which appropriation takes its starting point (care of oneself and others of one's kind) and also to the developmental sequence leading to the emergence of virtue and virtue-based happiness. The naturalness of these features is underlined by presenting them as the expression of nature's benevolent and providential care for animals and human beings.

The Stoic theory is also more universalist in approach than these other ancient theories. Appropriation is presented as a process that is characteristic of human beings as such, with partial analogues in the behaviour of other animals. Plato and Aristotle stress the importance of setting up the right kind of family, political and educational frameworks to enable ethical development. The Stoics, by contrast, present development as occurring in contexts that form part of human experience in general, such as engaging in family and community life, and (in Stoic terms) 'selecting things according to nature' and performing 'appropriate actions'.

What, exactly, does the Stoic stress on the naturalness of ethical development signify? It certainly does not mean that every single human being goes on to develop virtue and virtue-based happiness, as the Stoics understand these ideas. On the contrary, the Stoics emphasize that completing the full developmental sequence, as presented by Cicero in *On Ends* 3.16–22, is a rare and exceptional achievement, and belongs only to the ideal wise person.

Even so, the Stoics stress, the *capacity* to carry out this process is in-built in human nature and is one that can be realized in any family and social context. The scope for development is not ruled out by having an unfavourable upbringing or political framework. It is also important that the Stoics present ethical development as a process that forms part of adult, rational, life, and an ongoing one, not one that is completed during childhood and youth.

In effect, the Stoic account of appropriation is an ideal pattern, which we can all use as a basis for aspiration throughout our lives. We all have the core in-built dispositions (to care for ourselves and others of our kind) that form the starting points of development, and we can all use the Stoic ideal to shape the way that we conduct our adult lives to promote ethical progress towards this ideal. Also, as brought out in Chapters 5–6, the Stoics offer extensive guidance on relevant aspects of adult life, including practical deliberation about actions and the management of emotions and desires.

Ancient Stoicism is particularly rich in the guidance it provides for leading a better life in adulthood, in writings on practical ethics by thinkers such as Cicero, Seneca, Epictetus and Marcus Aurelius. The Stoic emphasis on this kind of guidance reflects their conception of ethical development as a natural process, open to all human beings, and carried out in the normal contexts of human life. In this respect, the Stoic theory of ethical development, especially their account of appropriation, in its various aspects, constitutes an especially valuable contribution to ancient, and, potentially, modern thought on this subject.

MODERN APPLICATIONS

The ancient Stoics were famous for the counterintuitive conclusions of their ethical theory, such as their claim that virtue is necessary and sufficient for happiness (examined in Chapter 1). Now we're confronted with another apparent paradox: virtue is natural, and yet we must learn to be virtuous. What did they mean by this? How could they say that virtue is natural when we see it so rarely in the people around us?

First, it's important to note that by 'natural' the Stoics did not mean 'ordinary' or 'average'. In many ethical discussions today, philosophers (and also psychologists) discuss what *most* people would do, or perhaps what they themselves would do. We tend to base our discussions of morality on our sense of what is normal and on the everyday behaviour we see around us.

In Stoicism, however, the normative person is the sage, or the ideal wise person. The ancient Stoics already knew how the average person behaved, and they were not impressed. They thought that many people were subject to bad emotions and did not live fulfilling lives. Rather than considering this way of living to be natural, they considered it *unnatural*—a misapplication of our capabilities as rational and sociable humans.

Living naturally, in contrast, meant aspiring to our highest nature, using our uniquely human gift of rationality to perfect our character.

While this level of ethical development is rarely achieved, it is still natural in the sense described above: it is the optimal pattern of growth for every normally functioning human being (exclusions apply for certain disabilities and incapacities). In the twenty-first century, we might say it's encoded in our DNA, the result of millennia of natural selection working on our species.

One aspect of the Stoic theory of appropriation (*oikeiōsis*) is locating human development in a broader natural context. (The ancient Greeks often achieved new insights about human nature by considering other elements of the natural world.) So, for example, we could say that every acorn has the capacity to grow into a mighty oak tree, but only a small fraction of them actually do. Many things could prevent an acorn from reaching its full potential: it gets eaten by a squirrel, it doesn't get enough water, it freezes in winter, and so on. Even those that do reach maturity may not attain their full potential in height, breadth and foliage. But some acorns *do* grow up to become majestic grandfather oaks. And when we think of oak trees in general, we tend to picture these beautiful specimens as the most characteristic of the species.

Likewise, the ancient Stoics thought that the most representative humans are those who come closest to our ideal: wise, just, courageous, self-controlled. Although not everyone reaches this ideal, that doesn't stop us from considering this to be the natural endpoint of a human life. The fact that full ethical development is not realized in every human being does not invalidate the Stoic view of the developmental process itself.

Unlike oak trees, of course, humans have personal agency that can help bring us closer to, or farther away from, our ideal. Even if we do not grow up in favourable conditions, or even when circumstances seem to be against us, we can still make every effort to develop towards a more fulfilling life. The ancient Stoics recognized that some settings are more conducive to promoting virtue than others; but they also believed that we can find ways to overcome disadvantages in our ethical background.

To take another somewhat simplistic analogy, but one which illustrates the idea well, let's think about physical health. Some people grow up in cultures or families where eating junk food is the norm, and as adults they may continue to eat a lot of junk food. However, since junk food is naturally unhealthy for humans, at some point they will begin to feel physically unwell. If they continue eating a significant amount of unhealthy foods, they will continue to deteriorate physically. If, however, they realize something is wrong and seek help, they can make positive changes in their lifestyle that will improve their physical health for the rest of their life.

In the same way, a continuous diet of bad behaviour – a stunting of our ethical development – will begin to damage our mental and emotional health. At some point we will recognize that we have a problem and need to make some changes. Given our natural human capacity for self-reflection and our desire for happiness, we have the ability to change our attitude and actions. The Stoic view of ethical development as an ongoing process in adult life can empower each individual to move closer to virtue and happiness in the present and future, regardless of what took place in their past.

Perhaps the contemporary approach that mostly closely resembles Stoicism in this respect is positive psychology, which is 'the scientific study of well-being and how to enhance it'.[13] Like Stoicism (and ancient virtue ethics in general), positive psychology values *eudaimonia* and tries to objectively evaluate evidence centred around human flourishing. Unlike Stoicism, however, positive psychology is wary of incorporating philosophical concepts like ethics and wisdom. Many researchers and clinicians shy away from the difficult ethical concepts that philosophy deals in. Instead, positive psychologists typically encourage clients to develop their strengths and passions in order to experience resilience, better relationships and deeper satisfaction with life.

Therefore, one promising path forward is for Stoic philosophers and positive psychologists to join forces, promoting an evidence-based but also ethics-based system of human flourishing. Stoicism could adopt the well-developed research apparatus of positive psychology, while positive psychology could adopt the coherent and cohesive Stoic ethical framework. We would all benefit from such a partnership!

Let's conclude this chapter with a brief word of caution. Although Stoics believe in lifelong ethical development, they also understand how difficult the process is. That's why they are firmly opposed to harsh judgements of anyone who does not complete the demanding transformation towards virtue. They consistently counsel patience, benevolence and understanding towards those who do not reach the endpoint – which is to say, all of us. As Marcus Aurelius says, 'It is a special characteristic of human beings to love even those who stumble' (*Meditations* 7.22). So while Stoic ethical theory is centred on the ideal pattern of *oikeiōsis* and life-long development, we should approach this ideal with both realism and compassion.

NOTES

1. IG: 128; LS 61 L.
2. IG: 113; LS 57 A.
3. Cicero, *The Nature of the Gods* 2.73–153, especially 2.112–19 (IG: 69–77, especially 74).
4. IG: 159; LS 57 E.
5. Cicero, *On Ends* 3.16–22 (IG: 151–3) (development of self-care); 3.62–8 (IG: 156–7) (development of care for others). See also Cicero, *On Duties* 1.11–15, which combines both kinds of care.
6. On Stoic thinking on human psychology, see Chapter 6.
7. IG: 113; LS 57 A. Cicero, *On Ends* 3.20 (IG: 152; LS 59 D(3)). Cicero, *On Duties* 1.12.
8. IG: 118–19; LS 59 E.
9. Cicero, *On Ends* 3.21–2 (IG: 152–3, LS 59 D(4–6)).
10. For these important texts, see also LS 59 D (IG: 151–3) and 57 F.
11. For these analogous features in the development of self-care and care of others, see Cicero, *On Ends* 3.20 and 3.62–3, 65 (IG: 152 and 156–7).
12. Cicero, *On Ends* 3.66, 68 (also 3.21–2, IG: 152–3).
13. LeBon 2014: 157.

FURTHER READING

T. LeBon, *Achieve your Potential with Positive Psychology* (London: Hodder & Stoughton, 2014).

J. Sellars, *Stoicism* (Chesham: Acumen, 2006), 207–9.

For more advanced study:

C. Gill, *Learning to Live Naturally: Stoic Ethics and its Modern Significance* (Oxford: Oxford University Press, 2022), Introduction to Part II, and ch. 4 (151–204).

S. Pembroke, 'Oikeiosis', in A. A. Long (ed.), *Problems in Stoicism* (London: Athlone Press, 1971), 114–49.

G. Striker, *Essays on Hellenistic Epistemology and Ethics* (Cambridge: Cambridge University Press, 1996), ch. 13.

Ancient writings:

IG: 113; LS 57 A

Cicero, *On Ends* 3.16–22 (IG: 151–3; LS 59 D)

Cicero, *On Ends* 3.62–8 (LS 57 F)

Cicero, *On Duties* 1.11–15

HOW DO WE LEARN TO MAKE GOOD DECISIONS?

INTRODUCTION

The next three chapters focus on deliberation about actions, on emotions, and interpersonal and social relationships. These are all subjects on which the Stoics have distinctive and original theories. However, in a broad sense, all three topics also form part of ethical development, the subject of Chapter 4. They are viewed by Stoics as part of the pathway by which we make progress towards virtue and virtue-based happiness, understood as the life according to nature.

The subject of this chapter is 'appropriate actions' (*kathēkonta*), a category explained shortly. An especially useful discussion is Cicero's *On Duties*, which provides guidance on performing appropriate actions; that is, in modern terms, practical deliberation or decision-making. There are several criteria for proper deliberation. However, the key criterion, as brought out in *On Duties* 1, is acting in line with the virtues. Thus, deliberation about practical actions is seen by the Stoics as part of the process by which we develop our understanding of the virtues and of how to live the best possible human life.

Deliberation about actions is also closely linked with 'selecting between indifferents', as explained in *On Duties* 2. Practical deliberation can involve making difficult choices, since acting rightly can conflict with gaining preferred indifferents, as Cicero brings out in *On Duties* 3. On both these aspects of decision-making, the crucial criterion is acting in line with virtue, and Cicero's guidance is designed to promote our understanding of what this criterion involves, as regards practical action.

'APPROPRIATE ACTIONS'

The topic of 'appropriate actions' is a standard one in the three ancient summaries of Stoic ethics. They are defined as actions 'which have a reasonable justification'; that is, actions for which good reasons can be given.[1] The category can be applied very broadly, to other animals, and even plants, as well as human beings. The term identifies actions which are appropriate for the form of life involved; Long and Sedley use the translation 'proper function' to bring out this idea.

In the case of adult human beings, the term refers to actions appropriate for animals which are distinctively rational and sociable. Typical examples include social actions, such as 'honouring parents, brothers and country, spending time with friends', and self-related actions, such as 'looking after one's health, and one's sense-organs'.[2] Actions of this kind are presented as always appropriate, whereas others are only appropriate under special circumstances. The considerations that can make an act appropriate are quite numerous, and depend in part on the circumstances of one's life, such as social situation, age or abilities.

This topic is often coupled with that of 'indifferents' in the three ancient ethical summaries. The two ideas are different in kind: indifferents consist of conditions of life (such as health or prosperity) that have positive or negative value, rather than types of action. However, both ideas reflect typical human, or animal, patterns of behaviour or motivation; and actions are often seen as appropriate because they promote preferable indifferents such as health, prosperity or a stable family life.

A further point of resemblance between the two categories is the relationship of both ideas to virtue. Actions can be more or less appropriate without reference to the virtue or vice of the person acting; and indifferents can have a positive or negative value without reference to virtue. However, whether or not appropriate actions or preferred indifferents contribute to a happy life, that is, the best possible human life, depends on the exercise of virtue, conceived as expertise in living. Hence, preferable indifferents such as health are not conceived as 'good', unlike virtue or virtue-based happiness. Similarly, the Stoics draw a distinction between 'appropriate actions' (*kathēkonta*), in general, and 'perfectly correct (or right) actions' (*katorthōmata*). The second kind of actions are 'perfectly correct', because they are carried out in a way that reflects the agent's virtue, that is, her expertise in living a good life.[3]

> The virtuous person's function is not to look after his parents and honour in other respects but to do so on the basis of wisdom. Just as the care of health is common to the doctor and the layman, but caring for health in the medical way is peculiar to the expert, so too the honouring of parents is common to the virtuous and non-virtuous person, but to do so on the basis of wisdom is peculiar to the wise person.[4]

This point marks a difference between 'appropriate actions' and the notion of 'duty' or 'right action', in much modern moral theory. Often, in contemporary thought, the moral quality of duties or right actions is defined without reference to the virtue or vice of the person acting. This point is discussed further shortly.

CICERO'S *ON DUTIES*: BOOK 1

For understanding Stoic thinking on practical deliberation, a very useful source is Cicero's *On Duties*. Although this is Cicero's own composition, it is closely based on Stoic writings available to him in the first century BCE. This is true of all Cicero's works on Stoic philosophy. But *On Duties* is an especially helpful text for modern readers; it is written in a highly accessible way and is full of suggestive practical examples. It is presented as a work of guidance to Cicero's son, then in his twenties and studying philosophy (as Cicero had done) at Athens. On this subject, then, Cicero's *On Duties* was intended to provide 'Stoic Ethics: the Basics' for his contemporary readers, most of whom were not experts in Stoic philosophy.

Book 1 of *On Duties* sets out the framework for Stoic decision-making; Book 2 discusses how to deal with preferred indifferents, which Cicero calls 'advantages' (*utilia*); and Book 3 examines cases of conflict between acting rightly and gaining advantages.

The main aim of Book 1 is to offer guidance on determining what is right (*rectum* or *honestum*, in Latin). The principal criterion is what is in line with virtue, supplemented by the idea of nature, meaning here human nature. In exploring what these criteria involve, Cicero refers extensively to more specific factors, especially family and social or political roles and situations. The general form of Cicero's guidance on decision-making resembles a framework offered by another important Roman writer on Stoic ethics, Seneca (first century CE). Practical guidance should be based, Seneca says, on a combination of general ethical 'doctrines' (*decreta*) and 'instructions' (*praecepta*) bearing on specific roles and contexts.[5]

Setting out criteria and procedures for determining what counts as 'right action' is also an important topic in modern moral theory. The criteria used include whether the action brings about a beneficial outcome or meets standards that can be applied universally. Typically, the criteria used make no reference to the virtue or vice of the person acting. However, Rosalind Hursthouse, an exponent of modern virtue ethics, defines right action by reference to virtue. A right action is what a virtuous person would do in the relevant circumstances, a view sometimes adopted by other theorists of virtue ethics. The Stoic approach is similar to that of Hursthouse. A right action is identified, primarily at least, as one which expresses virtue, given the relevant circumstances.

As noted earlier, the Stoics draw a distinction between appropriate actions, performed by people in general, and 'perfectly right actions' (*katorthōmata*), determined by the expertise of an ideally wise person. Cicero does not claim to be wise (nor did the heads of the Stoic school) and his guidance is not designed to provide definitive criteria for 'perfectly right actions'. His aim is the more modest one of providing criteria which make a given course of action 'reasonable' to adopt.[6] However, the ideal wise person and perfectly right actions provide the ultimate standard and the goal for ethical aspiration. By implication at least, what Cicero is offering is guidance which can help people to make 'progress' towards this goal.

CRITERIA FOR APPROPRIATENESS: VIRTUE AND NATURE

The overall structure of guidance in Book 1 is provided by the four cardinal virtues presented as covering the main areas of human experience. These are usually defined by the Stoics as wisdom, courage, justice and temperance or moderation. Cicero uses the variants 'greatness of mind' or 'magnanimity' (*magnitudo animi*) for courage, and 'fittingness' (*decorum*) for temperance; but he explains them in a way which includes the standard connotations of these cardinal virtues. Each virtue is described both in terms of its characteristic features and its actively beneficent, other-directed, dimension.[7] After offering a brief account of the virtue in question, Cicero offers specific illustrations of the kinds of action in which the virtue is expressed.

A second way in which Cicero specifies right action is by reference to the idea of nature, more precisely human nature (though elsewhere universal or cosmic nature plays an important role in Stoic ethics). Nature does not appear as a wholly separate or independent criterion; the two ideas, 'virtue' and 'nature', are interwoven and mutually supporting, as they are in the standard Stoic definitions of happiness.

In *On Duties* 1, human nature appears in three forms. First, we have a short account of human development, explaining that the four cardinal virtues constitute the developed expression of four primary inclinations, which reflect the distinctively human characteristics of being rational and sociable. Later, we find the idea that all human beings form a single broad fellowship or community (as naturally rational and sociable animals), which underpins more specific and localized social groups, including the family. A further idea is that, as human beings, we have four types of 'role' (*persona*), relevant for ethical life. Two of these express our nature and two express our specific social situation.[8] The opening account of development forms a starting point for Book 1 as a whole, in which the four virtues are used as the basis for guidance on right action. The function of the other two discussions of nature is explained shortly.

TWO EXAMPLES: GENEROSITY AND FOUR ROLES

Let us look more closely at two illustrations of Cicero's guidance in Book 1, on generosity and on the use of the four roles in connection with 'fittingness'.

The cardinal virtue of justice is analysed, like other virtues, in a twofold way. First, we have the distinctive features of justice (whose standard Stoic definition is 'knowledge in allocating what is due to each person').[9] Cicero stresses both respect for other people's rights and property and readiness to contribute to human fellowship and benefit by contributing one's own activities and resources. Second, Cicero offers advice on the actively beneficent dimension of justice, characterized as generosity or kindness, starting in this way:

> First, one must make sure that kindness harms neither the very people whom one seems to be treating kindly, nor others, next, that one's kindness does not exceed one's capabilities; and then, that kindness is bestowed upon each person, according to his standing. Indeed, that is fundamental to justice, to which all these things ought to be referred.
>
> (1.42)

The idea of adjusting one's kindness 'according to standing' is explained in this way.

We should consider someone's actions and attitudes towards us, the nature of our association and fellowship, and the services that the person has given us. It is in this connection that Cicero refers to the idea of nature. In a broad sense, all human beings have a shared fellowship (as rational and sociable animals); and so we should help anyone who is in need, including strangers and travellers. However, the fellowship of humankind also underpins our more specific associations, those within the family, friendship-group, community and nation. All these forms of association provide grounds for generosity on our part, which can be specified further by attending to the 'standing' of the person concerned.[10] Thus, Cicero's guidance combines a broad theoretical grounding (in the cardinal virtues and the idea of human nature) with procedures for reaching soundly based decisions in specific contexts.

The second illustration relates to 'fittingness' (*decorum*), the Ciceronian variant of the cardinal virtue of temperance or moderation. This virtue is normally seen in Stoic thought as expertise in the management of one's emotions, desires and behaviour, an idea also found in *On Duties*. This is combined, as in the other virtues, with a socially directed aspect, namely consideration and respect for other people, and sensitivity to the impact of our actions on their feelings and attitudes.[11]

The idea of the four roles provides both a broad theoretical basis for this virtue and also material for more fine-grained specification of its implications. Two roles are based on nature: our common human role as rational and sociable, and capable of developing the virtues; and our individual talents and inclinations. The other two roles consist in our specific social context in life, and our chosen project or career. Cicero's main point is that, if we are to achieve 'fittingness' in our pattern of motivation and our relationships to others, we should have regard to all these roles and work to achieve consistency and 'evenness' between them.[12]

Christine Korsgaard, a well-known modern moral thinker, has put forward the idea that, in making long-term and short-term decisions, we should take account of our 'practical identity', our social role and main project in life, as well as more general normative ideas, such as what it means to be properly human. The Stoic 'four roles' theory is similar to this idea, though the Stoic version is also closely linked with the idea of living according to virtue and according to nature.

Cicero also shows how putting this idea into practice can have profound implications. He cites the case of the Roman politician and general Cato (95–46 BCE), who felt that consistency with his personal character (the second role) demanded that he commit suicide after his defeat by Julius Caesar, rather than submit to Caesar's domination or 'tyranny'. Cicero presents his decision as a correct one, and one that was consistent with Cato's life-long character and policies, even though other generals, with equal moral validity, decided that their character and policies did not require such an extreme response (1.112). Here, and also in some of the examples in Book 3, Cicero brings out the potentially highly charged (life or death) implications of following Stoic guidance on virtue-based practical action.

CICERO, *ON DUTIES* 2

The subject matter of Book 2 is presented as the role of preferred indifferents, in Cicero's terms, what is 'advantageous' (*utile*), in practical deliberation. However, a more precise specification of the subject is needed to make sense of Cicero's discussion. What is examined here is the ethical status of advantages within a framework of decision-making which is centred on doing what is right (in line with virtue).

On Duties 1 is organized to show how the four cardinal virtues provide the basis for proper decision-making. By contrast, in Book 2, there is no attempt to present the advantages as providing an alternative framework for ethical deliberation. It is still assumed that, as in Book 1, the overall aim is to act in line with the virtues. The point at issue is how advantages fit into this project.

In fact, Cicero focuses, almost entirely, on one type of advantage, namely fame or reputation. The focus on fame or glory reflects its importance in Hellenistic and Roman aristocratic public life, especially for someone like Cicero, a leading orator and politician. However, the points made about fame also apply, to a large extent, to any advantage.

A key point is that the only valid, and reliable, basis for fame, is virtue. The virtue of generosity, when put into practice, produces a good reputation, in part, because generosity benefits other people, in public or private life. However, as Cicero stresses, the possession and exercise of the virtues, in themselves, attract admiration and respect:

> A vigorous love is aroused in the masses ... by the very reputation and rumour of liberality, of beneficence, of justice, of keeping faith ... the very thing we call right and fitting (*decorum*) pleases us in itself ... when we think people possess these virtues, we are compelled by nature to love them.[13]

The possession of 'greatness of mind' (magnanimity) in facing adversity, when some great and right actions are involved, has an inherent appeal for those who observe this and generates a good reputation. Although Cicero gives extensive guidance on the kinds of public and private actions that generate a good reputation, the underlying theme is that admiration is directed at the virtue itself, and not just the benefits provided by virtuous action.

In this kind of framework, what role does gaining advantages play in the motivation of the person acting rightly? Cicero puts it this way at one point: 'justice should be cultivated and maintained by every means, both for its own sake (otherwise it would not be justice), and for the sake of enhancing one's honour and glory' (2.42). This idea might have been expressed better by saying that 'justice is desirable both for its own sake and as the *only* justifiable means of gaining glory'.

In Stoic ethical deliberation, the motivation to act rightly (in line with virtues such as justice and generosity) must be the first priority. However, this does not exclude recognition that advantages such as fame have a positive value in themselves (though they are not good). Also, as Cicero emphasizes, public reputation, once acquired, also plays an instrumental role in enabling someone to exercise the virtues in public life. It is a standard part of Stoic ethical thinking that preferred indifferents constitute 'the material of virtue', that is, the means by which the expertise of virtue is expressed, as well as having positive value in themselves.[14] Thus, Cicero's guidance on the role of fame serves to illustrate Stoic thinking on the place of preferred indifferents in Stoic thinking on what counts as valid decision-making.

ON DUTIES 3

In Book 3, Cicero takes up the question how to deal with situations where there is a conflict between acting rightly and gaining advantages (or preferred indifferents). His aim here is not to put forward arguments for doing what is right, rather than advantageous. He assumes, from the framework offered in Books 1–2, that his reader is inclined to do what is right, whether it is advantageous or not. His aim is to provide guidance which can help a well-motivated person to deal properly with situations where there seems to be a clash between acting rightly and gaining advantage. Much of his discussion centres on case studies where this kind of conflict occurs. Some of the case studies are drawn from Stoic writings; others are composed by Cicero but approached from a Stoic standpoint. We consider two examples, one of each kind.

In 3.50–7, Cicero presents a debate between two successive heads of the Stoic school (Diogenes and Antipater) about the ethics of business dealings.[15] The debate centres on situations where you can increase your profit by keeping silent about facts which are relevant to buying and selling (the examples chosen are trading in corn and selling a house). Cicero presents the two heads as taking (partly) opposed positions on this topic. Diogenes advocates keeping silent about these facts, in line with normal business practice and what is legally required. Antipater advocates going beyond normal practice and disclosing all facts relevant to the sale, though these are not known by the buyer.

The two thinkers agree that one should do what is right, regardless of whether it is advantageous or not. Neither thinker advocates acting wrongly because it is advantageous. Their disagreement is about the course of action that meets this criterion. Antipater argues for a policy of maximal openness by reference to the Stoic idea of the fellowship of humankind:

> You should be considering the interests of human beings and serving the human community ... you have principles of nature ... to the effect that your advantage is also the common benefit, and conversely, the common benefit is yours. Will you conceal from human beings the material goods and resources that are available to them?
>
> (3.52)

Diogenes argues that, on this view, private property has no validity, and so 'nothing can be sold at all, but must be given' (3.53). Although the reported debate is not continued, Antipater could have replied that, even allowing for the legitimacy of buying and selling, the community of humankind demands openness in the way that this process is carried out.

The debate is interesting in several ways. First, it illustrates that the topic Cicero tackles in Book 3, how to act where acting rightly clashes with gaining advantage, was actively debated by Hellenistic Stoic thinkers. Second, it brings out that Stoic thinkers were prepared to recognize that certain kinds of case are difficult to resolve and are open to disagreement, even on Stoic principles. In some respects, Stoic ethical theory may seem very absolute and rigid, for instance, in the insistence that only virtue, and not the preferred indifferents, count as good. However, even so, the Stoics recognized scope for debate about how to apply these principles in specific situations. Third, it shows that the idea of the community of humankind was not only seen as a general ideal for aspiration but was deployed as a basis for action in specific cases, though its importance as a reason for action could also be disputed.

The second example is Cicero's own, and is based on earlier Roman history, but is fully in line with Stoic thinking. Regulus (third century BCE) was a Roman general, captured by the Carthaginians and sent back to Rome to negotiate his own exchange for several younger Carthaginian prisoners. On his return, he argued strongly against this exchange, which he said was not in Roman interests. Having sworn to the enemy that he would return to Carthage if he did not arrange this exchange, he did so, despite going back to certain torture and death (3.99–111).

The case is presented as a striking instance of someone who chose to do what he sees as right, even though it brought him no advantages, and involved his own death. He took the initiative in arguing against the exchange of prisoners, and in returning voluntarily to Carthage. The first decision was based on his judgement of what was best for his country, rather than for him. The second was based on his view of the importance of maintaining an oath given in a public context, even one given to enemies. Cicero presents both decisions as right and justified by the grounds given. Their rightness also consists in the fact that Regulus acted in line with the virtues, notably courage and magnanimity in opposing the exchange of prisoners, and good faith and justice in maintaining his oath.

Like the Stoic debate considered earlier, this is a case where there are legitimate grounds for taking different views on the rights and wrongs of the case. This point is brought out by Cicero's presentation of the issues, with arguments on each case, supporting or criticizing Regulus' decisions (3.100–8). Although Cicero supports Regulus' stance, he brings out in this way that a Stoic-style treatment can recognize the scope for ethical complexity and the difficulty in determining the right course of action in difficult situations.

Overall, Cicero's *On Duties* gives a full and reliable account of the way that the Stoics conceived ethical deliberation. The distinctive Stoic doctrine that only virtue, and not the preferred indifferents, count as good is reflected in Cicero's consistent emphasis on the importance of deliberating with the aim of doing what is right, that is, in line with virtue. At the same time, in Book 2, Cicero identifies a positive role for advantages in decision-making which reflects the mainstream Stoic view that preferred indifferents have inherent value (though not goodness). Also, he shows that the rigorous Stoic doctrine that only virtue counts as good is compatible with a recognition of ethical complexity and scope for valid debate about the right course of action in specific situations.

MODERN APPLICATIONS

In this chapter, we get to the heart of what most people would consider ethics: appropriate actions, especially towards other people. In the Stoic context, we've seen that the criteria of appropriate actions are based on a broad theoretical foundation, including the ideas of virtue, nature, and ethical development. Doing what is right depends on a whole worldview. Now that we have examined this background (in Chapters 1–4), we are ready to apply these ideas to determining what counts as appropriate actions in real life.

Many of us are used to thinking about our own everyday actions in terms of rules, from the Ten Commandments or the Golden Rule to the laws of our country. However, these guidelines have their limitations. A rule that makes sense in one situation (don't lie) becomes inappropriate in another situation (your lie will save someone's life). As Seneca points out, 'The same acts may be either honourable or dishonourable: what counts is why or how they are done' (*Letters* 95.43).

It is this *why* and *how* that Stoicism (and other types of virtue ethics) concerns itself with. An appropriate action is done for the right reasons and with the right disposition. These reasons may fluctuate from situation to situation. Seneca offers the example of someone sitting at the bedside of a sick friend. Usually we honour this as a caring and benevolent action, but if the sitter is simply hoping to receive an inheritance when the person dies, they are 'a vulture awaiting a corpse'. Although the act appeared noble and appropriate, the sitter's internal disposition rendered it inappropriate:

> An action will not be right unless one's intention is right, since that is the source of the action. The intention will not be right, in its turn, unless the mental disposition is right, since that is the source of the intention. Further, the mental disposition will not be optimal unless the person has grasped the laws of life as a whole, has settled on the judgements needing to be made about each thing – unless he has brought the truth to bear on his situation.
>
> (Seneca, *Letters* 95.57)

We can think this through for ourselves, using examples from everyday life. First, spend a few minutes trying to think of an ethical rule that could be followed in every applicable situation. When you come up with one, try to find a counterexample that would disqualify it. (For even more fun, hand your rule to someone else and see how many counterexamples they can find – we are all better at poking holes in other people's arguments.) Next, think of an example where someone follows a rule but for the wrong reasons (perhaps saying something that sounds right but for their own selfish ends). Finally, think of a time in your own life when you acted with good intentions but your actions did not have the result you hoped for. In this case, do you think you still acted rightly, even though your plans did not work out?

All these examples show why the Stoics believe we need virtue, not just rules or precepts, to guide our attitudes and actions. Why does virtue ensure appropriate actions? Because by aiming for virtue, we align ourselves with nature, directing our actions in a way that enables us to flourish as humans. It's not that we have a duty or obligation to act appropriately (as is assumed in deontological and consequentialist theories), but rather that acting appropriately produces the best outcomes for a species with our characteristics. The ancient Stoics believed that every species – dogs, horses, bees – has its own type of virtue, its own exemplary way of functioning. Given our human nature, virtues such as courage, temperance, and benevolence ensure optimal functioning for ourselves and our fellow humans.

While virtue can sometimes sound like an abstraction, it is made concrete in everyday life through our actions. As explained earlier in this chapter, Cicero provides a very helpful framework for thinking through our everyday behaviour in terms of Stoic appropriate actions. Epictetus also offers advice on *kathēkonta*, suggesting that appropriateness is not a one-size-fits-all proposition:

> To determine what is reasonable or unreasonable, not only do we have to form a judgement about the value of external things, but we also have to judge how they stand in relation to our own specific character.
>
> (*Discourses* 1.2.7)

He provides the striking example of an enslaved servant being made to hold out a chamber pot for his master. Will you refuse such a degrading act, Epictetus asks his students, and face a beating and starvation, or will you perform the act and have your supper? (For Epictetus this was not an idle question; he had spent the first part of his life as a slave.) It's just one in a series of ethical dilemmas he poses to his students throughout his lectures. Would you visit the home of a pompous rich person in order to ask for money? Would you play a humiliating role at the theatre because the tyrannical emperor asks you to? Would you betray a friend under threat of imprisonment and death?

These were all very real threats in imperial Rome, as they are today in many parts of the world, though they are ones which many of us today, thankfully, do not have to face. But we can still apply the same principles to our decisions right now. Like Cicero, Epictetus suggests that in order to act appropriately, we need to know our own character, our social roles (as a family member, citizen, professional, and so on), and what would be fitting in our particular circumstances. Rules and guidelines can be helpful, but they must be applied with good judgement based on our specific situation.

Let's briefly consider how some of this Stoic advice on appropriate actions might play out in contemporary life. For example, how would a modern-day Stoic approach the buying and selling situation debated by Antipater and Diogenes discussed earlier?

While most of us don't trade in corn these days, we do frequently buy and sell items through online forums. Imagine you are selling a used item (whether it's a guitar, a blender or a car) that appears to be in good condition but that you know has a significant flaw in its function. You know that a buyer will not be able to discover the defect just by looking at it, so you could conceivably try to sell it without disclosing the problem. Should you cover up the flaw and ask a higher price (then refuse any refund requests), or should you disclose the problem and ask a much lower price?

In this situation we would expect a seller to disclose any relevant information that impacts the product's function. The best policy is to provide all relevant information to the buyer and let them decide whether to proceed with the sale. Why would a seller be motivated to do this, when it clearly could result in a loss of sale or lower sales price for them? As Antipater insisted, 'You should be considering the interests of human beings and serving the human community.' By withholding important information or concealing a flaw, the seller would have harmed not only the buyer but also society more broadly – as well as the seller's own character.

Are there any situations in which it would be right for the seller not to disclose a flaw? It's possible. Perhaps if you were selling a car to a large used car retailer, who is purchasing the car from you as is, it would not be appropriate to disclose all the problems with your car. In that case, the buyer knows that most used cars have problems, and they are taking a calculated risk that buying large numbers of cars will even out their losses on any one particular car. If they ask for information about your car's defects, it would be right to provide all the information; you wouldn't want to lie or conceal. But depending on the terms of your agreement, it may not be necessary to explain everything that is wrong with your car.

Once again, rather than invoking an inflexible rule here, we find ourselves relying on thoughtful judgement and 'knowledge in allocating what is due to each person'. As Cicero emphasized, this includes an awareness of social conventions and expectations, as well as our own character and abilities. It may not be easy to codify appropriate actions into a simple maxim or precept, but this means that appropriate actions can be context-sensitive, dynamic and responsive to changing or nuanced situations; in other words, exactly what we need in our dynamic and constantly changing twenty-first century.

NOTES

1 IG: 136; LS 59 B(1).
2 IG: 118–19; LS 59 E(1–2).
3 IG: 1.136; LS 59 B(4).
4 LS 59 G(1–2).
5 Seneca, *Letters* 94–5 (LS 66 I–J).
6 Cicero, *On Duties* 1.7–8, 3.14–16.
7 On this point, see Chapter 3, pp. 43–44.
8 For these points, see Cicero, *On Duties* 1.11–15, 1.50–9, 107–15.
9 IG: 125 (standard definition); *On Duties* 1.20–2 (Cicero's version).
10 Cicero, *On Duties* 1.50–9.
11 IG: 127; LS 61 D(3) (standard definition); *On Duties* 1.99–104 (Cicero's version).
12 Cicero, *On Duties* 1.107–20, especially 110–11.
13 Cicero, *On Duties* 2.17, 32; also 37–8.
14 LS 59 A; Cicero, *On Duties* 2.36–50.
15 Diogenes lived in about 228–152 BCE; Antipater lived in about 200–130 BCE and was head during 152–130.

FURTHER READING

The key reading for this chapter is Cicero, *On Duties*. Two useful translations with introductions and notes are:

Cicero, On Duties, ed. and trans. M. T. Griffin and E. M. Atkins (Cambridge: Cambridge University Press, 1991).

Cicero, On Obligations, trans. with introduction and notes, P. G. Walsh (Oxford: Oxford University Press, 2000).

For more advanced study:

LS 59, on appropriate actions ('proper functions').

J. Annas, *The Morality of Happiness* (Oxford: Oxford University Press, 1993), 96–115.

T. Brennan, *The Stoic Life: Emotions, Duties, and Fate* (Oxford: Oxford University Press, 2005), chs. 11–13.

C. Gill, *Learning to Live Naturally: Stoic Ethics and its Modern Significance* (Oxford: Oxford University Press, 2022), ch. 2, especially 72–101, and 317–22.

B. Inwood, 'Rules and Reasoning in Stoic Ethics', in K. Ieradiakonou (ed.), *Topics in Stoic Philosophy* (Oxford: Oxford University Press, 1999), 95–127.

For right action and modern virtue ethics, see:

J. Annas, *Intelligent Virtue* (Oxford: Oxford University Press, 2011), 41–51.

R. Hursthouse, *On Virtue Ethics* (Oxford: Oxford University Press, 1999), ch. 1.

See also on 'practical identity':

C. Korsgaard, *The Sources of Normativity* (Cambridge: Cambridge University Press, 1996), 102–3, 105–7, 239–40.

HOW DO WE LEARN TO HAVE GOOD EMOTIONS?

INTRODUCTION

As stressed earlier, the Stoic idea of ethical development is both broad, taking in different areas of human experience, and cohesive, integrating these different aspects. In this chapter, the focus shifts from action and practical deliberation to emotion. First, Stoic thinking on emotion is related to their overall picture of human psychology. This helps to make sense of a striking feature of their theory, the contrast between misguided emotions or passions and 'good emotions'.

This contrast, in turn, is explained by reference to two aspects of Stoic thinking on ethical development. One is their explanation for human corruption, which affects emotions as well as actions. The other consists in their ideas about ethical development as a positive process. Crucial here is the theory of appropriation, examined in Chapter 4. Both strands in this process, the development of understanding and of relationships with others, are important for explaining their thinking on the difference between passions and good emotions.

The positive side of ethical development is sometimes described as the 'therapy' of (bad) emotions. The chapter ends by considering some examples of this process, which bring out the linkage between Stoic thinking on emotion, ethical development and therapy.

EMOTIONS AND HUMAN PSYCHOLOGY

Stoic thinking on emotion has often been criticized, from antiquity onwards. It has also been caricatured, as iron self-control (or 'the stiff upper lip') and as denial of the role and value of emotions in human life. Although the Stoics did, indeed, have strong and radical views about emotions, the exceptional nature of their thinking on this subject is often exaggerated.

In fact, most of the major ancient Greek theories (those of Plato, Aristotle and the Stoics at least) hold a broadly similar view about the role of emotions in ethical life. The virtuous person is seen in all these theories as someone whose emotions and desires are in line with her own sound ethical judgements, and who is internally coherent in this respect. However, this ideal is conceived by the Stoics rather differently from Plato and Aristotle; and this difference has given rise to misunderstandings of the Stoic view.

In Plato and Aristotle, we find a contrast that has become rather familiar, between 'reason' and 'emotion' or 'desire'. Emotions are seen as stemming from a distinct 'part' of the personality from reason; that is, a separate and independent source of motivation. The virtuous person is someone in whom emotions and desires are 'ruled' or 'harmonized' by reason. The Stoics conceive the personality (Greek *psuchē*) as functioning in a more unified or holistic way. In adult humans, emotions and desires are shaped directly by beliefs and reasoning.

The Stoics evolve a new terminology for this process. Their account of motivation applies, with modifications, to both human beings and other animals. Motivation, in animals (including humans) is analysed as a response to an 'impression' (*phantasia*), which can be a perception or a thought, that a certain action or reaction is 'appropriate'. This produces a 'motive' (*hormē*, often translated as 'impulse') to act or react in the way seen as appropriate. In this respect, at least, their approach resembles what is sometimes called the 'stimulus–response' model in modern psychology.

In adult human beings, the formation of motives is modified by the development of rationality. Rationality is understood as an interconnected set of capacities, including those for language and communication, logical reasoning and forming judgements. The emergence of rationality brings about two changes in motivation. First, 'impressions', covering perceptions and thoughts, are, or can be, formulated in terms of language, and take the form of beliefs or judgements. Second, adult humans need to give 'assent' or 'agreement' before the impression is accepted. However, once accepted, the belief directly or automatically produces the motive to act or react in a certain way.

In this unified picture of human psychology, reason and emotion do not constitute independent, and potentially conflicting, parts of the personality or sources of motivation. Emotions, which are seen as a subdivision of 'motives' (*hormai*), are shaped directly by beliefs or judgements. Although this picture is less familiar than the one based on the idea of distinct psychological parts, it resembles a well-known modern psychological model, the 'cognitive' one. In this model, emotions and desires are seen as based on 'cognitions', which (like Stoic 'impressions') cover a wide range of psychological functions. The cognitive approach to emotions is often adopted in contemporary psychology and theory of mind; the fact that the Stoics anticipate it gives their theory added modern interest.

STOIC DEFINITIONS OF EMOTIONS

This conception of human psychology explains why Stoic emotions are sometimes defined as types of belief and sometimes as types of motive, since both elements form part of their analysis of human emotion. The motive is often described in psychophysical terms, reflecting the Stoic view of psychological processes as, also, physical ones. The emotion involves being 'elated' (swollen) or 'contracted' by a certain belief; what is 'elated' or 'contracted' is the 'controlling centre' of psychological experience (*hēgemonikon*), which corresponds to the modern brain but which the Stoics locate in the heart.

To illustrate these features, let's look at two sets of definitions of emotions. These are definitions of generic types of emotion, which cover the main areas of human experience (rather like the Stoic four cardinal virtues, in this respect). The Stoics also recognize and define many specific emotions, which fall under these generic types of emotion, as they do with virtues. In these definitions, the first two emotions refer to things seen as good or bad in the future; the second two emotions (or one, in the case of good emotions) refer to things seen as good or bad in the present.

The first set of emotions are bad or defective, whereas the second set are good. The first set are called *pathē*, which is just the standard Greek term for 'emotions', though they are sometimes called 'passions' by scholars; the second set are 'good emotions' (*eupatheiai*). The first type of emotions form part of the experience of virtually all of us; they are 'emotions' as normally understood. The second set are experienced only by the ideal wise person (like the virtues). However, human beings are all naturally capable of achieving virtues and of experiencing good emotions, and we should aspire to doing so.

The reason why there are only three (not four) generic good emotions is because the virtuous person never experiences the only thing that is bad, in Stoic terms, namely ethical vice or defectiveness. As this indicates, the Stoic theory of emotions is not a purely psychological theory, without ethical connotations; the analysis of emotions (good and bad) forms an integral part of their ethical theory. However, the Stoics also believe that it matches the facts of human psychological experience.

Here are the two sets of definitions:

Bad emotions:
Desire (or appetite) (*epithumia*) is a (mistaken) belief that a future thing is good, such that we (irrationally) reach out for it.
Fear (*phobos*) is a (mistaken) belief that a future thing is bad, such that we (irrationally) avoid it.
Pleasure (*hēdonē*) is a (mistaken) belief that a present thing is good, such that we are (irrationally) elated at it.
Pain (or distress) (*lupē*) is a (mistaken) belief that a present thing is bad, such that we are (irrationally) contracted (or depressed) by it.

Good emotions:
Wishing (*boulēsis*) is a (correct) belief that a future thing is good, such that we (rationally) reach out for it.

Caution (*eulabeia*) is a (correct) belief that a future thing is bad, such that we (rationally) avoid it.

Joy (*chara*) is a (correct) belief that a present thing is good, such that we are (rationally) elated about it.

These definitions represent a slightly modified version of those we find in ancient sources, and are designed to underline the difference between the two sets. There are two main differences between the two sets of emotions. The first set ('emotions' as ordinarily understood) are based on mistaken beliefs about what is good and bad. They are based on what the Stoics see as the false belief that 'preferred indifferents' such as wealth and health count as really good. The good emotions are based on a correct understanding of what counts as really good and bad, namely virtue and vice.

The second difference is that the bad emotions are described as being 'irrational' whereas the good emotions are 'rational'. What does this difference consist in? 'Irrational', here, does not mean 'non-rational'. Both kinds of emotion involve beliefs or judgements about goodness or badness. They also involve a second judgement that it is right or appropriate to react in a certain way to what is seen as good or bad. Both kinds of judgement are needed, the Stoics think, to produce a motive. In this respect, both kinds of emotion involve the human capacity for rationality. Thus, in describing bad emotions as 'irrational', the term 'rationality' or 'irrationality' is being used in an evaluative or normative way.

What, then, makes a bad emotion irrational and a good one rational? There are two relevant differences. One is that the judgements involved in a bad emotion are ethically misguided. This applies both to the judgement about what is good and bad and the judgement that it is therefore appropriate to react in a certain way. The other difference is that the emotional response (the motive) is seen as being, in itself, an irrational psychological phenomenon; hence, Stoics sometimes describe a bad emotion as a 'sickness' of the psyche.

What do the Stoics have in mind here? The Stoics explain in this way striking features of emotions, as ordinarily understood. These are the fact that emotions are (at least sometimes) intense, or overwhelming; the Stoics compare them to running legs rather than walking ones. Emotions also sometimes come into conflict with other emotions or with the person's own better judgement. Hence, the Stoics characterize (bad) emotions as 'disobedient to reason' or as 'rejecting reason'. These are features which make bad emotions or passions 'irrational' and a form of psychological sickness.

EMOTIONS AND ETHICAL DEVELOPMENT

If bad emotions are a form of psychological sickness, why are they so widespread, while the good emotions are relatively exceptional? This is a question often raised about Stoic ethics more generally, since, in their view, virtue is a rare achievement. Even so, Stoics believe that 'all human beings have the starting points of virtue';[1] and so virtue and virtuous emotions are proper targets of aspiration for all of us. The means of making 'progress' towards these targets is ethical development; correspondingly, the Stoics have much to say about development, in connection with their theory of emotions, and in ethics generally. It is in connection with their thinking on emotion that we find the Stoic account of ethical corruption. When this account is taken alongside their theory of positive development, presented as 'appropriation', this goes a long way towards clarifying the differences between good and bad emotions and also explains why the experience of bad emotions is so widespread.

The Stoics offer a 'two-fold' analysis of the causes of ethical corruption. The first cause is the 'persuasiveness' of our 'impressions'; and the second is the 'influence of those around us'.[2] Underlying the first cause is the idea that 'preferred indifferents' such as health, wealth or fame have a natural appeal and are a source of pleasure for us. We naturally form the 'impression' that they are intrinsically good and that we should make them our overall objective in life. This 'persuasive impression' is confirmed by the 'influence' of those around us (parents, friends, society in general), who share this valuation of such things. This type of social influence is the second cause of ethical corruption.

In one account, this process is traced back to our early experience of pain and pleasure in birth and early infancy.[3] This leads us to over-value 'things according to nature', initially warmth rather than cold and physical pleasure rather than pain. In adult life, the things over-valued are preferred indifferents such as health, wealth and fame, which also have a natural appeal, which is confirmed by social influence. The cumulative effect of this process is to promote a misguided framework of judgements about what is good or bad and about how it is appropriate for us to act and react. Thus, the process of corruption shapes our overall pattern of emotions, making us inclined to experience bad emotions rather than good ones.

The corresponding positive account of ethical development is, primarily, the theory of appropriation. The first strand of this process, expressing care for oneself, is centred on progressive understanding of the relationship between the value of preferred indifferents and virtue. The process of selection between indifferents serves as a context for understanding that virtue (and happiness based on virtue) alone are good. Things such as health and wealth have positive value, and are normally selected by the virtuous person, but they are 'indifferent' compared with virtue. The second strand of appropriation, expressing care for others, involves the progressive widening and deepening of our relationships with other people. In conjunction with the first strand, this enables us to form relationships which are informed by virtue and by a correct understanding of the relative values of virtue and indifferents.[4]

The combination of these two accounts of development, positive and negative, explains, to some extent, the difference between (defective) emotions and good ones. These differences come out in the two sets of definitions, and in the Stoic accounts of the specific good and bad emotions that are grouped under the four generic headings. The widespread prevalence of the sources of corruption explain why defective emotions are so common, when taken in combination with the fact that completing the two strands of appropriation is an exceptional achievement.

In line with this framework of thinking about development, bad emotions are based on the mistaken belief that preferred indifferents are good. Emotions such as fear (for instance, fear of death), anger, jealousy or passionate lust stem from attaching goodness not to virtue, but to the preservation of life at all costs, or social status, or erotic pleasure; that is, things that are, at most, 'preferable'. Bad emotions also often involve negative or hostile attitudes towards other people, such as spite or hatred. This partly reflects over-attachment to preferred indifferents, but also a failure to develop properly the in-built human disposition to care for others in the way we conduct our relationships.

By contrast, the good emotions show the outcome of proper development, in analogous respects. In place of 'fear' (for one's life, for instance), we find 'caution'. This is not a watered-down version of fear; the caution is directed at avoiding actions which are ethically wrong. In place of 'desire', we have 'wish'; and most of the specific types of this generic good emotion take the form of good will or affection towards other people. In place of 'pleasure', we find 'joy', particularly joy as a response to good actions, one's own or someone else's, or to the order and coherence of the universe. The accounts of good emotions thus represent the outcome of completing the two strands of appropriation. These two strands are centred on the development of ethical understanding and of properly conducted relationships, respectively; and ethical development as a whole combines these two strands.

The Stoic accounts of ethical corruption and appropriation also explain a second feature of their presentation of good and bad emotion, the contrast between 'rational' and 'irrational' emotions. A key feature of this contrast is the difference between psychological stability and coherence (good emotions) and instability, internal conflict and lack of coherence (bad emotions).

In Stoic thought, virtue and virtue-based happiness are often associated with qualities such as order, consistency and coherence. These qualities are those of someone acting and feeling in line with the four cardinal virtues, as a unified or interdependent set. Correspondingly, Stoic descriptions of the later stages of ethical development stress the progressive increase of these qualities as one moves nearer to virtue and happiness.[5] Similarly, the good emotions of the virtuous person (generically, wish, caution and joy) also reflect the coherence, stability and order of her understanding and character; this can be described as a form of 'rationality'.

By contrast, the defective emotions express a character and life that lacks this kind of coherence. These emotions tend to be localized or intermittent, responding in a short-term way to the events of the moment. At the same time, they are often urgent and forceful or overwhelming, expressing the mistaken judgement that what is desired or shunned at any given moment is good or bad, and that one's happiness in life depends on getting or avoiding them.

Emotions of this kind tend to come into conflict with each other, since they reflect judgements that do not form a coherent framework. They may also conflict with the person's better judgement, either on another occasion, when she is not in the grip of emotion, or even at the time of feeling the emotion. This kind of emotional pattern also militates against forming stable and caring relationships with other people, of the kind that are promoted by the social side of ethical development. These are all features that the Stoics emphasize in defective emotions, and which contribute to the idea of them as 'irrational'.

In all these ways, Stoic thinking about the contrast between good and bad emotions closely reflects their ideas about ethical development and the sources of corruption.

DEVELOPMENT, THERAPY AND EXAMPLES

Stoic thinking about ethical development and its failure explains why bad emotions are so prevalent. At the same time, the Stoics insist that all human beings have the in-built capacity for ethical development, and hence for experiencing good emotions. This underlies their interest in the idea of the 'therapy' or cure of (bad) emotions, an idea which the Stoics took a lead in formulating, though it became a widespread one in ancient ethical thought and practice. The Stoic therapy of emotions serves as a means of counteracting failures in ethical development and thus correcting, or at least modifying, the tendency to experience bad emotions. The idea of the therapy of emotions plays a significant part in Stoic theoretical writings and informs their writing on practical ethics, in thinkers such as Epictetus and Marcus Aurelius.

As brought out earlier, the Stoics see emotions as based on evaluative beliefs or judgements, in this respect prefiguring the modern 'cognitive' theory. This approach recognizes the scope for modifying emotions by correcting the beliefs on which they depend (this is also a feature of modern 'cognitive' psychotherapy). Thus, we find evidence that some Stoic thinkers discourage people distressed by grief from thinking that grieving is something they should necessarily regard as appropriate or right. Tackling the underlying belief is seen as a way of modifying the emotion. Another technique advocated is dwelling in advance on future possible disasters and thus being better prepared emotionally if disasters do occur.[6]

In Epictetus' *Discourses*, especially, we find methods designed to counteract the tendency to feel bad emotions. Epictetus often stresses that our emotions depend on the judgements we make in response to events, and not on the events themselves. He also urges people to 'examine' their 'impressions' (thoughts, perceptions) before giving 'assent' to them, to ensure that their emotional responses are based on sound judgements. He also urges us to refrain from applying the judgement that a given fact or event is good or bad, since such judgements generate (often bad) emotions.[7] These methods all reflect standard features of Stoic thinking about the causation of bad emotions; and his advocacy of them constitutes a contribution to their therapy.

In considering Stoic therapy, we focus on two aspects which illuminate in different ways their thinking on emotions and ethical development. One is the use of the figure of Medea as a cautionary example of bad emotion or passion. The other is Marcus' presentation in his *Meditations* of good emotions as something to aspire towards, thus promoting the therapy of bad emotions.

THE STOICS AND MEDEA

The mythical figure of Medea was most famously presented in Euripides' fifth-century BCE tragedy. She is widely used by Stoic thinkers to illustrate bad emotions, and to accentuate the need for the therapy of these emotions. Medea's presentation by Euripides is marked by several striking features. She exhibits a range of intense, overwhelming emotions including jealousy and anger, leading to violent actions, culminating in the murder of her own children to punish her husband Jason for abandoning her to make a more advantageous marriage. She is highly articulate about the emotions she is experiencing and her grounds for these emotions and the actions she takes.

Especially interesting for the Stoics is the tragic monologue in which she speaks about her own internal conflict and self-division. Her decision to kill her children to take vengeance on her husband comes into sharp conflict with her own love for her children. As she puts it in these climactic lines: 'I understand that what I am about to do [kill the children] is bad, but anger masters my intentions, anger which is responsible for the worst things in human life.'[8]

It is clear why the Stoics use Medea as a cautionary example of bad emotion and failure in ethical development. As Epictetus points out, she is misguided in thinking that taking vengeance on her husband is more beneficial than saving her children's lives.[9] In Stoic terms, she regards taking vengeance and restoring her honour (a preferred indifferent, at best) as something that is intrinsically good and that determines her happiness in life.

Also, her emotional responses exhibit several marks of 'irrationality', as understood by the Stoics, including intensity and overwhelming force, and sudden shifts of mood and intention. The poetic lines just quoted illustrate this irrationality very clearly. At first sight, these lines, expressing conflict between Medea's judgement about what is bad and her anger, support a Platonic–Aristotelian psychological model (with distinct and competing 'parts') rather than the Stoic, more unified, conception. However, the Stoics see this representation of Medea as one which illustrates and supports their ideas about the psychological effects of defective emotions.

As the Stoics interpret her lines, Medea herself recognizes and spells out the internal conflict that the Stoics see as characteristic of the 'irrationality' of bad emotions. The nature of this conflict is best viewed in the light of Stoic thinking on ethical development as appropriation. Medea's decision to kill her children is 'bad' (for her as well as the children) because it runs counter to her love for her children, which the Stoics take as the key indicator of the disposition to care for others that is in-built in all human beings. Thus, although Medea has developed (badly) into someone whose character is marked by emotional and physical violence, she retains this primary human motive, which provides the potential for enabling her to become a better person. Even Medea, the extreme case of violent emotion, shows that she has 'the starting points of virtue'.[10]

Although Medea, in theory at least, could be the object of therapy, the primary targets of Stoic discussions of this figure are other people, especially those who are more obviously disposed to make progress towards virtue. For them, Medea serves as a cautionary example of bad emotion, which shows how such emotions can be highly damaging for the person concerned as well as for others; such emotions constitute a kind of psychological sickness that needs to be cured.

MARCUS AURELIUS: THERAPY AND GOOD EMOTIONS

The overall project of Marcus' *Meditations* is that of promoting his own progress towards virtue and virtue-based happiness by reflecting on core themes of Stoic ethics. In doing so, he conveys to himself that ethical development brings with it the tendency to experience good, rather than bad, emotions; in effect, he carries out the therapy or cure of bad emotions in his own case. Here are three examples of this process.

In one passage (2.1), Marcus counteracts the anger and resentment that might be provoked by other people's behaviour by reminding himself that they are fellow-members of the community of human beings, as rational and sociable animals. By implication, he carries out the therapy of bad emotions such as anger, by promoting the corresponding good emotion of good will or good intent (an attitude he commends often in the *Meditations*).

In Book One of the *Meditations*, Marcus reviews the positive qualities whose value he has come to understand by his experience of people who have been important in his life. These qualities include freedom from bad emotions and an inclination towards good emotions. Here is one such comment: his friend Sextus 'never gave the impression of anger or any other passion but was at once completely free of passions and yet full of affection for others' (1.9.9). In taking Sextus as his model, Marcus is, in effect, taking forward his own therapy from anger and other passions and promoting the development of contrasting good emotions such as affection.

A further notable feature of the *Meditations* is that Marcus confronts his own approaching death with a kind of joy, rather than fear, and combines this attitude with good will or affection for those left alive, even if they have been hostile or critical of him. This passage, written late in the collection (and thus likely to be close to his own death) is an example:

> I am leaving the kind of life in which even those who were close to me, for whom I toiled, prayed and took so much care, even they want to see an end of me ... [addressing himself] you must not, however, on that account, depart thinking less kindly of them, but preserve your true character as one who is friendly, well-intentioned and gracious.
>
> (10.36.4, 6)

Marcus contrasts the hostility of his critics with 'kindness' or good will (a good emotion). He aspires at least to reciprocate their negative emotional attitude with his positive and well-judged one. His reflection is designed, again, to carry out the therapy of the bad emotion he might otherwise experience and its replacement with an equivalent good one.

In these three features, Marcus encapsulates the linkage between ethical development, therapy, and the two kinds of emotion that forms a striking dimension of Stoic thinking.

MODERN APPLICATIONS

In popular culture, and in some schools of psychology and philosophy, emotions are seen as experiences outside of our control: mental events that happen to us, rather than ones we create for ourselves. Many people believe negative or positive emotions are determined by external situations; if you win the lottery you will automatically feel elated, and if you are in a car accident you will automatically feel sad and angry. Strong emotions, especially when expressed outwardly, are seen as markers of authenticity or depth of character. In this view, our emotional life is bound to be turbulent because we are at the mercy of what happens to us in an unpredictable world.

Stoicism asks us to question this supposedly common-sense view of emotion. Emotions are mental experiences that result not directly from external events, but from our *interpretation* of external events. As Epictetus says:

> It isn't the things themselves that disturb people, but the judgements that they form about them. Death, for instance, is nothing terrible, or else it would have seemed so to Socrates too; no, it is in the judgement that death is terrible that the terror lies. So accordingly, whenever we're impeded, disturbed, or distressed, we should never blame anyone else, but only ourselves.
>
> *(Handbook 5)*

Socrates faced death (by poison, at the hands of his fellow Athenians) calmly and without fear, which implies that fear of death is not inevitable. If we don't see death as harmful, then we will not be afraid of it. In some settings, such as the battlefield, people see death as something they need to accept for the sake of a worthwhile aim, the defence of their own country, families and friends. This means that it is our values and judgements that determine our emotions, not the external event itself.

This decoupling of emotion from external events permits a radical inner freedom. We are not 'pulled like puppets by our motives', as Marcus Aurelius says (*Meditations* 6.16), but we can have positive emotions even when we're beset by difficulties and hardship. It all hinges on our values. If you adopt the Stoic view that money, fame, popularity and even health are all indifferents, then there is no need to get upset if you don't have any of these things. You can still pursue *eudaimonia* through developing a rich inner life, centred on the recognition that virtue is the only really good thing. But if you adhere to a conventional mindset that assumes money and other indifferents are goods, and that your happiness depends on them, then you will naturally be sad, frustrated, resentful, jealous or angry if you can't get them.

We can illustrate the idea that emotions depend on judgements with examples from everyday life. Have you ever changed your mind about something or someone? Perhaps you had a negative first impression of someone, but after you spent more time with them, you realized they had some very worthwhile qualities. In this case the person didn't change, but your judgement of the person changed (you got to know them better and came to appreciate their character). Or maybe you didn't like a certain type of food, such as broccoli or green vegetables generally, but you realized it was a healthy thing to eat and gradually came to like the taste. Once again, the thing itself didn't change, but your opinion of it changed and led to an alteration in your emotion (I like broccoli) and motivation (eating broccoli helps me to lead a healthy life). At a more fundamental level, when we change our minds about what is important in life and what makes us truly happy – in other words, our values – we change our emotions and motivations.

What about the competing Platonic–Aristotelian model that pits rationality against emotion or desire? Don't we sometimes feel that our desire for that delicious-looking brownie overpowers our rational resolution to stick to a healthy diet? According to the Stoics, this is not a battle between reason and emotion but between different values. If you value good health over immediate pleasure, then you will keep your resolution in mind to avoid eating the brownie. If you are not completely convinced that long-term health is more valuable than your enjoyment in eating the brownie right now, you are probably going to eat the brownie.

The same applies to negative emotions like fear or anger, which result from misjudging the value of external things. When we feel conflicted, or when we act against our own better judgement, we're not entirely committed to the values we claim to hold. Seneca explains this phenomenon in the context of acting courageously on the battlefield, which he thinks depends on not seeing death as a bad thing:

> No action can be honourable unless the mind is entirely set on its object, with no reluctance in any part of itself. When a person goes after something bad, either because he fears something worse or because he has other goods in view that make it worthwhile to absorb one bad thing, his judgements as an agent are at odds with each other. On one side is the judgement that bids him pursue his aims; on the other is the judgement that pulls him back and makes him shun whatever he suspects is dangerous. So he is torn in different directions, in which case glory is lost to him.
> (*Letters* 82.18)

In other words, if we *sort of* believe that death is not a bad thing, but we still have some doubts about this, we will find ourselves fearful when facing our own death. Or if we haven't truly committed ourselves to the idea that our good lies in eating healthy foods, we will easily slip up and eat the brownie. It's not a battle between reason and emotion but a stand-off between competing sets of values.

You can probably think of times when you've experienced this for yourself. Maybe you didn't want to do something, but you knew you really should do it. Or perhaps you knew you shouldn't get angry or upset about something, but you did anyway. Try to identify the competing values that pulled you in different directions in these situations. Why do you think it was difficult to choose (subconsciously) between the two different values?

Stoics believe this model represents a more accurate description of our psychological experience than the Platonic model. There are also practical advantages to seeing all our psychological functions (judgements, motivations, emotions) as part of a unified system. Rather than our emotions being at war with our rational mind, good emotions can form a valuable part of our personality and can have a rational basis. And instead of being controlled by our emotions, we can manage them by bringing them into alignment with our values.

NOTES

1 IG: 128; LS 61 L.
2 IG: 114.
3 Calcidius, *Commentary on Plato's Timaeus* 165–6. See Graver 2007: 154–7.
4 Cicero, *On Ends* 3.20–2, 62–8 (IG: 152–3, 156–7); see Chapter 4.
5 See, e.g., Cicero, *On Ends* 3.20–2 (IG: 152–3).
6 Cicero, *Tusculans* 3.28–31, 3.52, 3.76–7.
7 Epictetus, *Handbook* 1, 5. See also 'Modern Applications' on this point.
8 Euripides, *Medea*, 1078–80, concluding the monologue (1021–80).
9 Epictetus, *Discourses* 1.28.7.
10 IG: 128; LS 61 L.

FURTHER READING

B. Inwood, *Stoicism: A Very Short Introduction* (Oxford: Oxford University Press, 2018), 84–7.

J. Sellars, *Stoicism* (Chesham: Acumen, 2006), 114–20.

For more advanced study:

Ancient writings on emotion:

LS section 65.

C. Gill, *Learning to Live Naturally: Stoic Ethics and its Modern Significance* (Oxford: Oxford University Press, 2022), ch. 5.

M. R. Graver, *Stoicism and Emotion* (Chicago: Chicago University Press, 2007), especially chs. 1–3 and 7.

On modern theories of emotion and Stoicism:

M. C. Nussbaum, *Upheavals of Thought: The Intelligence of Emotions* (Cambridge: Cambridge University Press, 2001), chs. 1–2.

On modern applications:

W. Johncock, *Beyond the Individual: Stoic Philosophy on Community and Connection* (Eugene: Pickwick, 2023), ch. 6.

M. Pigliucci, *How to be a Stoic: Ancient Wisdom for Modern Living* (London: Penguin, 2017), ch. 12.

D. Robertson, *How to Think Like a Roman Emperor: The Stoic Philosophy of Marcus Aurelius* (New York: St. Martin's Press, 2019), chs. 6, 7.

HOW SHOULD WE RELATE TO OTHER PEOPLE AND SOCIETY?

INTRODUCTION

The proper conduct of interpersonal and social relationships does not appear as a distinct topic in ancient summaries of Stoic ethics, unlike most of the subjects considered so far in this book. However, Stoic philosophy offers innovative and valuable insights on this subject, though these sometimes appear in connection with other topics, for instance the social strand of ethical development conceived as 'appropriation'.

This chapter focuses on four interconnected questions: (1) How does Stoic thinking relate to modern ideas about altruism? (2) Does the Stoic approach to emotion advocate detachment from other people, as is sometimes supposed? (3) Does the Stoic idea of the community of humankind involve the devaluation of other types of social relationship? (4) In what sense do the Stoics engage in political theory? Although these questions raise distinct theoretical issues, they are also closely connected with each other, as well as with Stoic ethical theory more generally. Overall, the Stoics place a high value on ethically well-grounded involvement in interpersonal and social relationships, though they do so in a way that sometimes differs from modern expectations or the approaches of other ancient theories.

STOICISM AND ALTRUISM

Modern thinking on interpersonal relationships tends to be centred on a contrast between egoism (identified with selfishness and pursuit of one's own self-interest) and altruism. Special value is attached to pure altruism, in which no benefit is conferred on oneself, or to generalized altruism, in which the person benefited is not closely connected with oneself. The egoism–altruism contrast plays an important role in modern moral thinking; indeed, the term 'moral' is often identified with 'altruistic'.

It is sometimes assumed that the egoism–altruism contrast is equally important in ancient Greek and Roman ethical frameworks; and scholars often use it to interpret ancient ethical theories, including that of Stoicism. However, closer examination does not bear out this assumption. Actions and attitudes benefiting others are often given positive value; but they are not necessarily conceived in terms of the egoism–altruism contrast. In Greek and Roman culture generally, the ideas of reciprocity and 'the shared life' are more prominent than that of altruism.

Typically, in Greek ethical philosophy, the key normative ideas are virtue and happiness, rather than altruism. Certainly, as Julia Annas has pointed out, virtually all ancient theories 'find room for other-concern', either as part of their accounts of virtue and happiness or in connection with friendship (or, more broadly, interpersonal bonding, in Greek *philia*). However, virtue and happiness can be conceived in terms that are self-related or other-related (or neither, specifically), without this being seen as problematic.[1]

Also, when we find an ideal that seems close to altruism, it is sometimes qualified in ways we may find problematic. Aristotle, for instance, presents 'wishing the friend well for the friend's sake' as a salient mark of the best kind of friendship, based on shared virtue. However, he goes on to argue that exercising this kind of other-benefiting friendship also, at a deeper level, benefits the person herself. Acting as a friend of this kind benefits us by enabling us to express our essential self (as a virtuous agent) and thus to extend our own virtue-based happiness.[2] For Aristotle, this is an unproblematic addition to his argument, but from a modern standpoint, it rather undermines the positive value he places on other-benefiting friendship. We sometimes find a similar line of thought in Epictetus;[3] but it is not otherwise characteristic of Stoic thought.

In its overall approach to this subject, Stoicism is broadly similar to other Greek theories. The key normative ideas are virtue and virtue-based happiness, which can be seen as self-related, or other-related, or both. The egoism–altruism contrast is not one that is fundamental for Stoic thought. However, there are certain respects in which Stoic thinking, though differently framed from modern thinking, comes closer to the modern ideal of altruism than do other Greek theories.

One is the presentation of care for others as a motive that is just as primary and in-built in human beings as care for oneself. In fact, the Stoics see this as an instinct built into animals generally; but in human beings this motive is extended to a range of other people including, but going beyond, one's family and community. Indeed, it can be extended to people falling outside one's country, in the distinctive and exceptional Stoic idea of the community of humankind.[4] This extension of care to people not directly linked with us marks a special point of contact with modern ideas of altruism.

This feature of Stoic thought can also be linked with the presentation of human beings as, by nature, sociable as well as rational. This view of what is distinctive about human beings underpins the idea of the community of humankind. Although the notion of human beings as rational and sociable also appears in Aristotle (*NE* 1.7), it is more firmly embedded in Stoic thought.

The Stoic treatment of virtue also brings their thinking close to the idea of altruism. Of the four Stoic cardinal virtues, two (courage and justice), typically, benefit other people, rather than oneself. Given the Stoic theory of the unity or interdependence of the virtues, this means that the whole virtue-set has an overall other-benefiting focus. Also, in Cicero's *On Duties* 1 at least, all four virtues are presented as having other-benefiting dimensions, in addition to their standard connotations.[5]

As regards the virtue–happiness relationship, there are several relevant features, which come out more clearly by contrast with Aristotle.

For Aristotle, happiness depends not just on the exercise of virtue but also on things such as one's health, prosperity and the wellbeing of one's family. Also, Aristotle presents the highest kind of happiness as that which is based on purely intellectual or theoretical activity, rather than practical action which may benefit others. For the Stoics, by contrast, happiness depends on the exercise of virtue, taken on its own, and virtue, as just highlighted, typically has an other-benefiting dimension.[6] Also, the Stoics do not follow Aristotle (and Plato) in presenting theoretical or intellectual activity as superior to practical action as a basis for happiness or as the highest kind of happiness.

In these various respects, Stoic ethical thinking comes closer than other ancient theories to the modern valuation of altruism, even though the Stoic framework of thinking about interpersonal relations is not based on the egoism–altruism contrast.

STOIC DETACHMENT?

There is a rather widespread impression that the Stoic approach to emotions involves adopting an attitude of detachment from close relationships with other people. This view is surprising, in the light of several important features of Stoic thought, reviewed shortly. It is largely based on a single passage (in two versions) in Epictetus, quoted and discussed later. However, this passage, if placed in its context, does not bear out the impression that Stoicism encourages emotional detachment.

As explained in Chapter 6, the emotional attitudes advocated by Stoicism are the 'good emotions', which are the outcome of the two strands of ethical development, conceived as 'appropriation'. The second (social) strand of appropriation takes its starting point from the in-built human motive of care for others, typically exemplified by parental love. The full expression of this motive includes a wide range of types of relationship, including engagement in family and communal roles, and care for any given human being, as a fellow-member of the community of humankind. The complete realization of this strand also involves the development of ethical understanding, which forms the first strand of appropriation, and the expression of this understanding in and through interpersonal and communal relationships. The ideal outcome of this process is not detachment from other people but full-hearted social engagement combined with ethical understanding.[7]

This view of the outcome of ethical development is borne out by examination of the various emotions which are listed as specific subtypes of the generic emotion-types, both bad and good, in Stoic theory. Many of the bad emotions listed in our sources consist of negative or hostile attitudes to other people, whereas many of the good emotions involve positive attitudes. For instance, the generic emotion of pleasure has subdivisions including 'spite' (delight at things that go badly for someone else), and the generic emotion of desire includes various forms of hatred. By contrast, the generic emotion of joy includes joy in a good person's actions (those of oneself or someone else), while the generic emotion of wish includes various forms of good will and 'cherishing' (*agapēsis*) suggesting affection or love.[8] This analysis confirms the view that the Stoics see ethical development as leading not to detachment but to ethically well-judged involvement.

A revealing text for this purpose is Seneca's dialogue, *On Peace of Mind*. The main theme of this work is that the best way to gain peace of mind is through sustained and committed engagement with one's chosen social or political role. This engagement provides the basis for confronting life's adversities, including danger and death, without loss of peace of mind. Seneca's work incorporates the idea of the four roles, including one's chosen role of project, which is prominent in Cicero's *On Duties*, but adapts it for this different purpose.[9] Again, there is nothing to suggest that the Stoics recommend emotional detachment as a basis for securing one's own peace of mind.

Against the background of these Stoic ideas, it is puzzling that some scholars highlight emotional detachment from close interpersonal relationships as a Stoic ideal. In fact, there is just one passage, in two versions, that is regularly quoted to support this idea: Epictetus, *Discourses* 3.24.88, which forms the basis for *Handbook* 3. Let us focus on the *Discourses* passage, which comes with an explanatory context, unlike the passage from the *Handbook*:

> From now on, whenever you take delight in anything, call to mind the opposite impression: what harm is there in your saying beneath your breath as you're kissing your child, 'Tomorrow you'll die'? Or, similarly to your friend, 'Tomorrow you'll go abroad, or I will, and we'll never see each other again'.

On the face of it, these words are shocking, and they support the common view about Stoic detachment, at least in this case. However, they need to be placed in context. They occur in a dialogue between Epictetus and a former student from Athens, now based in Rome where he is a senator for life and involved in public affairs. The former student is anxious about leaving his home city to carry out his work because of his concern that one of his family or friends might die while he is away. He maintains that he cannot show proper family feeling or friendship if he leaves his home to fulfil his political role in Rome.

Epictetus' advice, in response, is similar to Seneca's in *On Peace of Mind*. This is that the person concerned should carry through the social and political role he has undertaken, as senator, assuming it is ethically worthwhile. He should not be distracted from doing this by anxiety about the death of family members or friends while he is away or about the impact of his own death on absent family or friends. He should accept that death is a permanent, natural, part of human existence; and that we need to live our own lives, and conduct our relationships, in consciousness of this fact.[10]

This is the context of the lines quoted. Epictetus is not saying that we should stop loving and caring for our friends and family. He is saying that we should continue to love them (he uses the word for 'love', *philein*, several times in this context),[11] while remaining conscious that our relationship to them (or theirs to us, if we die first) can be ended by death at any point. The idea that, as human beings, we need to be aware of our mortality, is a recurrent theme in Stoic thinking (for instance, in Marcus' *Meditations*), and in other Greek theories, notably Epicureanism.

Epictetus' image of someone thinking about death when kissing a child or parting from a close friend is a disturbing one, and deliberately so. However, it is not clear that the image is designed to encourage detachment from the other person. Epictetus may, rather, be saying: *although* you are (rightly) attached to someone, you should still remind yourself of the permanent possibility that the relationship will be broken by death. This interpretation matches the general stress in Stoic thought on the value of (well-judged) interpersonal and social engagement. On this reading, Epictetus' passage confirms, rather than contradicts, the general Stoic advocacy of ethically informed involvement with other people.

THE COMMUNITY OF HUMANKIND

The idea that human beings form a broad family or community is a distinctive and innovative theme in Stoic ethical thought. Closely related ideas are that the universe (or *kosmos*) provides a context for this human community, of which we are co-citizens (Stoic cosmopolitanism).[12]

How does this idea fit with the stress in Stoic thought, illustrated in this chapter, on the value of well-judged involvement in conventional forms of interpersonal and social bonding, those of family, community and nation? Should we see Stoic cosmopolitanism as superseding other forms of commitment, or as representing the highest ideal, for which other forms of engagement are a kind of preparation or preliminary? This interpretation is sometimes offered by scholars. Also, Stoic thinkers were sometimes criticized in antiquity for giving equal weight to concern for strangers and foreigners as to family, friends and co-citizens.[13]

However, closer examination of several Stoic treatments of this theme suggests a rather different view. Stoic cosmopolitanism does not replace or invalidate other forms of bonding; rather, it builds on them or enhances them. It adds an additional layer of significance, but one which does not negate the ethical significance of other types of relationship.

For instance, in his account of the social strand of appropriation, Cicero identifies two main rational expressions of the primary motive to care for others. One is a readiness to engage in family and community life and the other is a recognition of humanity as forming a broader kind of community. In the same context, he uses two contrasting figures to exemplify the best form of social engagement: the hero Heracles who performs services for the whole human race, and the ideal wise person who expresses his virtue through involvement in family and community life. The two pathways are presented as equally valid alternatives.[14]

In a partly parallel discussion (*On Duties* 1.50–3), after considering the principles underlying human association (rationality, sociability, and the capacity for virtue), Cicero identifies the community of humankind as the widest expression of these principles. He cites as a typical expression of this community our readiness to help those in need (such as strangers and travellers), wherever they are from. He goes on to identify more specific forms of human association (those of nation, region and family). These are also presented as reflecting these underlying principles, without suggesting that they have a lower ethical status.

Two other Stoic discussions introduce new themes, but without changing the overall position. Cicero reports a debate on buying and selling between two heads of the Stoic school, Diogenes and Antipater. Whereas Diogenes, in line with conventional practice, argues that the seller does not need to reveal defects that the buyer is not aware of, Antipater maintains that the seller should take the initiative in disclosing these defects. Antipater appeals to the idea of the community of humankind in support of doing so; he uses this idea as a ground for adopting standards of interpersonal conduct that go beyond conventional practice. However, Antipater does not call into question the validity of buying and selling as such; in this sense he maintains conventional norms.[15] The Stoic ideal is used to justify a localized revision of normal practice, not to invalidate conventional forms of ownership.

The second Stoic discussion is Hierocles' use of the image of circles of relationship, and his advocacy of contracting the circles. The outermost circle is that of human beings as such; Hierocles urges us to draw each circle in, by one circle; thus, we should treat any given human being as if they were a member of our own state. This is part of a general policy of extending the scope of our concern for others.[16] Like Antipater in the previous discussion, Hierocles is urging a partial revision of conventional practice or attitudes by reference to the community of humankind. However, his revision presupposes the validity of conventional social bonds, and uses them as the basis of the extension of our concern. Again, the discussion sees as compatible the ethical validity of the idea of the community of humankind and of conventional social groups.

Two further examples develop, in rather different ways, the idea that we are members of two kinds of state, our political nation and the universe, treated as a kind of state. Seneca uses this image to refer to the contrast between leading a life of political involvement and one of philosophical theory, including understanding the nature of the universe and its ethical significance. He argues that both options are valid, in Stoic terms, as long as both kinds of life are used virtuously and in a way that benefits others; thus, the Stoic heads benefited humankind by their philosophical activity (that is, by being citizens of the universe, in this sense).[17]

Marcus Aurelius uses the image slightly differently: 'As Antoninus [his Roman family name], my city and fatherland is Rome, as a human being it is the universe. It is only what benefits these cities which is good for me.'[18] What Marcus has in mind is, first, performing his local role, as emperor, by the highest (normal Roman) standards. At the same time, he aspires to live by the highest human standards, which are, in Stoic terms, also those of the universe as a whole. Here, Marcus refers to the idea that virtue and virtue-based happiness involve living the best possible human life which is also in line with the best principles of the natural universe.

In suggesting that he aims to benefit *both* states, Marcus conveys that he aspires to meet both standards by the same kind of activities; that is, being a good emperor and a good human being.

So, for both Seneca and Marcus, the ideal of cosmopolitanism (being a citizen of the universe) is ethically compatible with leading an engaged political life. Cosmopolitanism does not replace engagement in normal, conventional states, though it adds a new layer of understanding of the ethical principles underlying our social involvement.

Overall, then, there is a clear pattern in these discussions. The ideal of the community of humankind or cosmopolitanism is used to enhance our understanding of the principles of social engagement and not to supersede or replace conventional types of involvement.

STOIC POLITICAL THEORY

Did the ancient Stoics engage in political theory? The answer to this question is not entirely straightforward. This is not only because the Hellenistic Stoic writings on this subject do not survive and are only known about indirectly. There seems to have been a significant difference between Stoic thinking on this topic and the approaches of earlier Greek thinkers.

The most famous political works of the fourth century BCE, Plato's *Republic* and *Laws*, and Aristotle's *Politics*, combine three strands. (1) We find debate about the merits and demerits of different types of constitution, such as democracy, aristocracy and monarchy. (2) There are ideas about the best, ideal or near-ideal, constitution. (3) There is reflection on the ethical principles underlying all forms of political association, especially the best or ideal state.

Of these three types of political theory, the first, on constitutions, is quite absent from Stoic thought, and the second, on the ideal state, is found only in an exceptional form. The focus is, almost entirely, on the third strand, the principles underpinning political association or community. These are, to a large extent, the same principles that underlie Stoic ethics, more generally, including its social aspects. In this sense, it is open to question whether we can identify a distinctively *political* dimension in Stoic thought.

The best-known Stoic work on politics is Zeno's *Republic* (Chrysippus also wrote a work with this title), which seems to have been a response to Plato's famous *Republic*. Though known only from later evidence, it seems clear that Zeno does not describe an ideal constitution, by contrast with Plato's *Republic*. Indeed, he seems to have maintained that political constitutions or social institutions are not ethically significant in themselves. What matters is whether or not those involved have virtue, especially wisdom, and live in concord, friendship, and love towards each other. In effect, then, Zeno's 'republic' is a community of the wise, not one of a normal kind (nor is it the broader idea of the community of humankind).[19]

In its rejection of conventional social structures and forms, Zeno's work is often seen as influenced by Cynicism, a radical philosophical movement in this period. However, the focus on core underlying ethical principles, rather than on constitutional form, remains the hallmark of Stoic theory in this area. For instance, we know that Chrysippus wrote extensively on justice and law. However, his subject was justice and law in general, not these principles seen as underlying, or embodied in, specific types of state or social structure.[20] Stoic ideas about justice and law were derived from their thinking about human development as appropriation, or about rationality as a property of both human beings and god or the natural universe. Thus, political theory is merged with social theory or the social dimension of ethics.

Why did the ancient Stoics not engage in theory about constitutional structures as Plato and Aristotle had done? Stoic thinkers were not a-political or anti-political in the way that the Epicureans were, their Hellenistic contemporaries and rivals. Stoic thinkers regarded involvement in politics, as well as family and community, as a normal part of a full human life.

However, the broader political context for Stoicism was very different from that of Plato and Aristotle. Until the late fourth century BCE, Greek states (which were small city-states) were self-governing, with a wide variety of constitutional forms. Throughout the whole history of Stoicism, as an active philosophical movement (third century BCE to second century CE), Greece was dominated either by the successors of the Macedonian Alexander the Great or by Rome, though political life of a kind continued within city-states under their rule. The Stoic response was not to advocate individualism or a-political quietism. The Stoics encouraged involvement in whatever political context one found oneself in, regardless of the constitutional framework. The key point was living according to ethical principles, those of justice, or the virtues, or reason and sociability, whatever one's political situation. If it proved impossible to maintain those principles, the Stoics advocated withdrawal from politics. The Stoics also believed that those principles could be followed effectively in non-political activities, for instance, by being a philosophical teacher or engaging in family and community life more broadly.

Consistently with these ideas, we find Stoic teachers or adherents of Stoicism playing a variety of political roles. They might act as advisers of Hellenistic kings or of Roman emperors (such as Seneca, adviser of Nero), or as emperors themselves (Marcus Aurelius). They might be leading politicians in the Roman republic, such as Cato; or philosophical teachers, whose students often entered political life, such as Epictetus.

Roman Stoics sometimes played a prominent role as critics or opponents of politicians aiming at sole rule or emperors. For instance, Cato opposed Julius Caesar when he aimed to take over as sole ruler of Rome; Cato also committed suicide rather than surrender to Caesar. However, on Stoic grounds, their opposition was not based on the idea that imperial rule as such was wrong or that the Roman republican constitution was right. It was based on the conviction that certain emperors or leading politicians were committing criminal acts, and that this justified opposing them or, if need be, ending your own life, rather than colluding in their injustice.[21]

Thus, overall, Stoic political theory and practice are consistent, and have a coherent rationale, though it differs from other, more well-known, forms of political theory.

MODERN APPLICATIONS

In contrast to ethical systems in which socially beneficial behaviour is imposed from the outside by rules or laws, Stoicism holds that humans are instinctively affectionate towards others. We are social creatures, predisposed to cooperate with and care for other people. This is not considered a matter of philosophical speculation but an empirical fact that can be validated by observation: humans everywhere are seen to live in groups and care for the people they live with. (You can investigate this premise for yourself by thinking about whether humans always live in groups, whether humans can survive for long without other people, and what happens in cases of social isolation, such as solitary confinement.)

Given that we are social by nature, the question is not *whether* we care for other people but *who* specifically we care for and *how* we care for them. For example, we might ask questions like: do we care for only the people nearest to us (family and close friends), or a broader group like fellow citizens, or do we care for every person on the planet? What should our interactions with them look like? How do we engage with other people, both as individuals and as a society?

Stoicism helps us answer these questions by framing our relationship with other people in terms of human fellowship and the community of humankind. Seneca explains this position nicely when he says:

> Nature brought us to birth as kin, since it generated us all from the same materials and for the same purposes, endowing us with affection for one another and making us companionable. Nature established fairness and justice. According to nature's dispensation, it is worse to harm than to be harmed. On the basis of nature's command, let our hands be available to help whenever necessary.
>
> (*Letters* 95.52)

Stoicism sees all humans as inherently possessing dignity and being worthy of care and consideration. While we can shape our characters in better or worse ways, every human remains worthy of care simply because they are human (even violent murderers like Medea, discussed in Chapter 6). This also means we don't divide the world into 'us' and 'them'. We shouldn't think that our own family, community, tribe or nation is superior to others. In this respect, Stoics are impartial: we know our own family and friends are not inherently better than other people or entitled to special treatment.

In other ways, however, Stoics are not impartial. We are not expected to give up our close personal relationships in order to care equally about everyone in the world. In fact, these relationships with our family, friends and community members are some of our richest and most valuable experiences as humans. We love our family and friends, knowing they are important to us without thinking they are more important than other humans. We should not try to benefit our loved ones by harming other people.

This social ideal of caring about everyone – but caring in particular ways for particular people – is difficult and demanding. We have a natural instinct for care, but it takes ethical maturity to care *wisely*. The ancient Stoics thought we are naturally capable of progress over our lifetime towards ideals of justice and benevolence (see Chapter 4 on ethical development). But this process doesn't always go smoothly; it is often disrupted in some way, resulting in the immature expression of our social instinct.

One way this instinct can be misapplied is through social insularity: we may sincerely love our family and friends, but not give due consideration to people we don't know. In this case, we need to practise extending our care to people farther away from us. So, for example, we find Marcus Aurelius urging us to 'Love the human race' (Meditations, 7.31) and Hierocles exhorting us to feel kinship with people who are distant from us (as discussed earlier in this chapter).

On the other hand, we may make mistakes with people closer to home too: not appreciating our close friends and family members; getting frustrated or angry when people do things we don't like; becoming resentful at the way others treat us; worrying too much about what other people think of us. We may also love people in a grasping or possessive way, or fear losing them – which is the mistake Epictetus tries to correct with his advice about remembering our loved one's mortality.

All of these are ways we misapply our natural tendency to care about other people. Have you seen any of these mistakes in action, either in yourself or others? Do you find it more difficult to extend your care to people you don't know, or to act with unflagging kindness towards people you do know (who may annoy you or break your heart)? These are both difficult ethical challenges. The great advantage of Stoic ethics is that it recognizes the importance of both challenges and offers some practical solutions for overcoming them.

That's why the ancient Stoics, in their practical writings, explain how we can learn to care wisely for others. One way of doing this is by developing virtues like generosity and benevolence, as when Epictetus says that the wise person 'will always be frank and open with one who is like himself, and will be tolerant, gentle, forbearing, and kind with regard to one who is unlike him'. An ancient summary of Stoic ethics asserts that 'the virtuous man is affable in conversation and charming and encouraging and prone to pursue goodwill and friendship through his conversation'.[22] Other socially directed Stoic virtues include being affectionate, cheerful, encouraging, lovable, loving and public-spirited.

As you can see, contrary to stereotypes of the detached or anti-social Stoic, Stoicism is an intensely pro-social philosophy that advocates both cosmopolitanism and rewarding personal relationships. The ancient Stoics took for granted that we *do* care for other people, so they focused on ways to expand and perfect our social instincts. Promoting Stoic ethics in the twenty-first century can motivate people to become socially engaged members of society who are also committed to the broader community of humankind.

NOTES

1 Annas 1993: 223–6.
2 Aristotle, *NE* 8.2–3, 9.4, 8, 9.
3 Epictetus, *Discourses* 1.19.11–15, 2.22.19–21.
4 Cicero, *On Ends* 3.62–8 (LS 57 F, IG: 156–7), *On Duties* 1.50–3.
5 On these points, see Chapter 1, pp. 16–17, Chapter 3, pp. 43–44.
6 Aristotle, *NE* 1.8–10, 10.7–8. On Stoic thinking on virtue and happiness and the contrast with Aristotle, see Chapter 1.
7 See Chapter 4, referring especially to Cicero, *On Ends* 3.16–22, 62–8 (IG: 151–3, 156–7; LS 59 D, 57 F).

8 See Graver 2007: 56, 58; also Chapter 6, pp. 93–94.
9 Seneca, *On Peace of Mind* 6.1–3; Cicero, *On Duties* 1.107–21.
10 Epictetus, *Discourses* 3.24.84–92.
11 Epictetus, *Discourses* 3.24.86–7.
12 Cicero, *On Ends* 3.63–4 (IG 157); LS 67 L.
13 LS 57 H.
14 Cicero, *On Ends* 3.62–8, especially 3.66, 68 (IG: 156–7, LS 57 F).
15 Cicero, *On Duties* 3.50–7; see also Chapter 5, pp. 79–80.
16 LS 57 G.
17 Seneca, *On Leisure* 4.1, 4.4–6 (LS 67 K).
18 *Meditations* 6.44.5.
19 LS 67 A–E.
20 LS 67 R–S.
21 On Stoic opposition to Roman emperors, Griffin 1976: 360–6.
22 Epictetus, *Discourses* 2.22.36; IG: 147.

FURTHER READING

This chapter covers a wide range of topics and there is no obvious single overview available.

For more advanced study:

Relevant ancient writings:

LS 57 and 67.

J. Annas, *The Morality of Happiness* (Oxford: Oxford University Press, 1993), especially 223–6 and ch. 12.

C. Gill, *Learning to Live Naturally: Stoic Ethics and its Modern Significance* (Oxford: Oxford University Press, 2022), 204–10, 226–46, 273–8.

M. T. Griffin, *Seneca: A Philosopher in Politics* (Oxford: Oxford University Press, 1976), 360–6 (on Stoic opposition to emperors and its basis).

M. Schofield, 'Social and Political Thought', in K. Algra, J. Barnes, J. Mansfeld, and M. Schofield (eds), *The Cambridge History of Hellenistic Philosophy* (Cambridge: Cambridge University Press, 1999), 739–70.

On specific good and bad emotions, including those directed at other people:

M. R. Graver, *Stoicism and Emotion* (Chicago: Chicago University Press, 2007), 56–9.

On modern applications:

D. Fideler, *Breakfast with Seneca: A Stoic Guide to the Art of Living* (London: Norton, 2022), chs. 10, 12.

W. Johncock, *Beyond the Individual: Stoic Philosophy on Community and Connection* (Eugene: Pickwick, 2023), ch. 4.

D. Robertson, *Stoicism and the Art of Happiness* (London: Hodder & Stoughton, 2013), ch. 5.

8

WHAT DOES STOICISM CONTRIBUTE TO MODERN VIRTUE ETHICS AND LIFE-GUIDANCE?

INTRODUCTION

In this chapter and the next, we consider the relationship of Stoic ethical ideas to certain areas of modern thought and practice. In this chapter, the areas are modern virtue ethics and what is often called 'life-guidance', then in the next chapter, environmental ethics. We are highlighting these areas of contemporary thought because they are ones where Stoic ethics has made a significant contribution or could do so.

The two areas considered in this chapter are rather different in kind. Virtue ethics forms part of contemporary academic philosophy, whereas life-guidance is directed at a broad public audience. However, the two areas overlap in content. Also, the features of Stoic ethics that enable it to make a significant contribution to both areas are similar, although they are treated differently in the two contexts. These features include Stoic thinking on the virtues and the virtue–happiness relationship, as well as on practical decision-making, emotions and interpersonal relations. The rich resources of Stoic ethical guidance are especially important for life-guidance but are also potentially valuable for modern virtue ethics.

In both areas we set the scene by outlining the contemporary context and then highlighting the contribution of Stoic ideas; in virtue ethics this contribution is largely potential so far, but in life-guidance a substantial contribution has already been made.

ANCIENT AND MODERN ETHICS

Readers of this book coming from a study of modern moral theory may find many of the ideas rather unfamiliar and surprising. There is a marked contrast between the dominant approaches in modern moral theory and those of Stoicism and ancient ethics more generally. However, recent developments in modern thought have provided an opening for Stoic ethics to contribute constructively to contemporary moral debate.

The focus in modern ethics, at least until recently, has been on right action, rather than on the qualities of agents. The criteria of right action are, typically, what counts as a duty or obligation, on the one hand, or what confers human benefit, on the other. In both cases, formulating rules or procedures, as a basis for decision-making, is a central concern. Rules are established either by universalization (can this rule be applied in all cases?) or by working out the likely consequences of certain types of action and determining how beneficial they are.

The dominant theoretical frameworks have tended to be either Kantian (for duty-based approaches) or consequentialist, especially Utilitarian (for approaches centred on human benefit). Modern moral theory is, typically, centred on promoting actions that benefit other people, rather than oneself; and interpersonal ethics is often framed in terms of a binary contrast between egoism and altruism. Also, ethics is often subdivided between normative theory, centred on determining standards or rules, and applied ethics, linking the theoretical frameworks with specific areas of practice or specimen cases.

On virtually all these points, there is a marked contrast between modern ethics and the approach typical of ancient ethics, including Stoicism. The central focus in ancient thought is on the qualities and standpoints of agents, rather than on right action. The formulation of rules is not a major concern. The key question is what counts as good, rather than what is right, especially what constitutes virtue and happiness (*aretē* and *eudaimonia*, in Greek), taken as embodying goodness.

Human psychology is also a central topic, especially the question of the type of motivation and emotional attitudes characteristic of virtue or happiness. Another ancient concern that does not have the same prominence in most forms of modern ethics is with ethical development, conceived as the process by which people progressively acquire virtue and happiness. A related question is whether accounts of virtue or happiness can be supported by reference to nature, either human nature, or nature as a whole, or both.

Similar contrasts apply in the case of self–other relations. Ancient thinking on this topic is not centred on a binary contrast between egoism and altruism. Virtue and happiness can be conceived as self-related, or other-related, or as combining these. Although other-benefiting actions and attitudes are positively valued, ethics is not seen as, primarily, other-benefiting rather than self-benefiting. Also, in ancient ethics, the boundary between ethical theory and guidance on practical action is less marked than in most modern ethics. Since the standpoint of the agent is more central, theoretical reflection about virtue or happiness is seen as capable of directly affecting our actions and attitudes.

In recent years, the gap between ancient and modern ethics has been narrowed by the revival of moral theory centred on virtue ('virtue ethics', as it is often called). Early exponents of this approach were often highly critical of standard modern forms of moral theory and advocated their replacement by virtue ethics. Later exponents have tended to maintain that virtue ethics should be treated as a valid alternative to theories centred on duty and human benefit. Some thinkers have also argued that virtue ethics can accommodate ideas that are central to other approaches, such as right action, or a focus on other-benefiting actions, but reframed in terms of virtue.

In contemporary moral theory, there are at least two strands of virtue ethics. One strand aims, explicitly, at a modern version of ancient ethics, especially as found in Aristotle; this strand is sometimes called 'Neo-Aristotelian' virtue ethics. This approach incorporates the main features of ancient ethics, especially the central roles of virtue and happiness, and sometimes sees accounts of human nature as supporting ethics. Thus, it constitutes a combination of virtue ethics, eudaimonism (theory of happiness) and ethical naturalism.

Other contemporary thinkers centre ethical theory on virtue and the qualities of agents, rather than actions; however, they do not treat happiness as a key expression of goodness. They do, however, sometimes cite human nature and natural human feelings as support for virtue-centred ethics. These thinkers tend not to take ancient thinkers such as Aristotle as their models, referring instead to earlier modern philosophers such as Hume or Nietzsche. A further strand in modern theory recognizes that virtue is a significant ethical idea, but sees it as playing a supporting role in approaches centred on duty or human benefit.

As this discussion indicates, the situation in contemporary ethical theory is quite fluid and complex, with various approaches being regarded as valid and actively explored. A further factor is the emergence of new areas of moral theory, such as environmental ethics. This situation gives scope for fresh appraisal of the value of Stoic ethics, as a positive contributor to modern debate.

STOICISM AND MODERN VIRTUE ETHICS: VIRTUE AND HAPPINESS

Within modern virtue ethics, Stoicism is closest to the 'Neo-Aristotelian' strand, which gives a central role to ideas about virtue, happiness and in some cases human nature. Both Aristotle and Stoicism offer powerful models for modern virtue ethics. The advantages of Aristotle's approach are already well-known; the alternative merits of the Stoic theory are less often appreciated, and can usefully be set out here, based on the detailed accounts of Stoic ethics in Chapters 1–7.

Stoicism offers a highly unified, coherent and systematic theory of ethics, centred on the role of virtue in human life. Virtue, when fully developed, is seen as shaping all other aspects of human life, including actions, emotions, and interpersonal and social relationships. This point has an obvious relevance for an approach (modern virtue ethics) in which virtue is the central concept and main bearer of value.

The question on which Stoicism and Aristotle diverge most sharply is the scope of what counts as 'good'; this is closely linked with the question of the relationship between virtue and happiness.

For the Stoics, virtue alone is good (along with things dependent on virtue), and happiness depends solely on virtue. Aristotle too regards virtue as a prime expression of goodness; but he also recognizes as goods things such as health, prosperity, and the welfare of family and friends. He sees goods of the second kind, as well as virtue, as needed for happiness. The rival merits of these two positions were much debated in ancient philosophy.[1]

Some modern virtue ethical thinkers tend to adopt Aristotle's position on this point, rather than the Stoic one.[2] However, the Stoic view has significant advantages. It makes for a more unified and consistent theory, which is more systematically based on the goodness of virtue. The Stoic innovative concept of 'indifferents' recognizes the positive value for human life of things such as health and prosperity, without giving them the primary ethical value (goodness) that belongs to virtue and things based on virtue. The Stoic approach explains more clearly the importance of virtue for happiness, which both theories accept, and integrates the two ideas (virtue and happiness) in a more unified theoretical framework.

VIRTUE, HAPPINESS AND NATURE

This point is reinforced if we bring in the role of nature in the two theories. Aristotle refers to human nature to support his definition of happiness as 'activity according to virtue' (*NE* 1.7). Later in the *Nicomachean Ethics* (10.7–8), Aristotle uses the contrast between human and divine nature to endorse his presentation of theoretical activity, rather than practical, as constituting the highest kind of happiness. Scholars have sometimes seen this second move as inconsistent with the first, or, at least, seen the two uses of the idea of nature as not fully integrated with each other.

In Stoic ethics, as brought out in Chapter 3, ideas of human and universal nature are used repeatedly to support Stoic claims about the virtue–happiness relationship. In comparison with Aristotle's usage, the conceptions of human and universal nature are more thoroughly integrated with each other and with the Stoic analysis of virtue, happiness, and the virtue–happiness relationship.

The idea of nature, both human and universal, is further integrated in Stoic thinking through their distinctive and innovative theory of ethical development as 'appropriation' (Chapter 4). This theory, taken on its own, is potentially of value to modern virtue ethics as an alternative to the Aristotelian view of ethical development. Considered as a whole, Stoic ideas on ethical development, the virtue–happiness relationship and nature offer a powerful conceptual model for modern virtue ethics. These ideas have a special relevance for those modern theories, such as those of Philippa Foot and Rosalind Hursthouse, in which the ideas of virtue and happiness are seen as integrated with, and supported by, an understanding of human nature.

CONCEPTIONS OF VIRTUE

Both Aristotle and the Stoics aim at presenting an ethical theory which matches human beliefs and practices in general. However, the Stoics are prepared to diverge further from conventional ideas, for the sake of producing a more theoretically coherent and systematic account. For instance, Aristotle stays close to conventional ideas in the range of qualities he recognizes as virtues. The Stoics, by contrast, organize the virtues into four groups, using what were generally recognized as the four main or 'cardinal' virtues (wisdom, courage, justice and temperance or moderation) as generic types. They present these four cardinal virtues as covering the four main areas of human experience. They follow a similar typological approach as regards the emotions.[3]

This approach has advantages for formulating conceptions of virtue whose validity can be recognized in different cultures and time-periods. Aristotle's range of virtues include some, such as 'magnificence' or 'magnanimity', which are framed in strongly culture-specific terms.[4] The Stoic approach to virtues is more universalizing and less culture-specific. The Stoic universalizing approach to ethics is also evident in other respects, for instance, in their concept of the community of humankind, an idea whose ethical appeal is still evident to us.

A similar point applies to the Stoic idea of virtue as skill or expertise in living, which underpins their claim that virtue (as distinct from indifferents) confers benefit, consistently and unconditionally.[5] The idea of virtue as expertise is not part of Greek conventional thought, and is not adopted by Aristotle. However, it is a theoretically powerful idea, and has been taken up by some thinkers in modern virtue ethics.

VIRTUE AND RIGHT ACTION

A further topic on which Stoicism is especially helpful is one that has been much debated in modern virtue ethics. This is the question whether virtue ethics can find room for the notion of right action that is central for most other kinds of modern ethical theory. A view sometimes proposed (by Hursthouse) is that, in virtue ethics, right action is defined as the kind of action a virtuous person would do, in the relevant circumstances.

Stoic ethical theory on decision-making, as presented in Cicero, *On Duties*, offers an illuminating parallel for this idea. Cicero accentuates features of our interpersonal or social relationships that make a specific kind of action a duty or obligation. However, he also stresses the importance of performing this action in line with virtue (one of the four cardinal virtues); in addition, he shows how reference to the idea of human nature can specify or reinforce the ethical significance of a given action. He offers extensive guidance on how to use these criteria for decision-making in particular situations.[6]

This is a point of convergence between Stoic and modern virtue ethics that has no obvious parallel in Aristotelian ethics; it illustrates the relevance of the Stoic approach for modern theory as well as practice.

STOICISM AND MODERN VIRTUE ETHICS: CONCLUSION

The points discussed here do not exhaust the features of Stoic ethics that are significant for modern moral thought, especially in virtue ethics. Another relevant feature is that, while stressing the other-benefiting dimension of ethics, especially in connection with virtue, Stoic thought offers an alternative to the modern binary contrast between egoism and altruism.[7] However, this discussion illustrates the wide range of topics on which Stoicism is well-placed to contribute to modern virtue ethics.

LIFE-GUIDANCE: BACKGROUND

What is 'life-guidance', and what is the background for the substantial contribution of Stoic ethics to this area of modern life?

By contrast with much modern 'applied ethics', which offers guidance directed at specific areas, such as business or medicine, life-guidance offers advice on the management of one's life overall. Recent years have seen an upsurge of books, courses and online resources in this area, especially in Western countries such as the USA and UK. It is plausible to connect this development with the waning influence of traditional sources of such advice, such as churches, the family and political movements. Life-guidance has often been based on various ethical or religious frameworks, including Buddhism; however, in recent years, Stoicism has become a major source of such guidance.

Various factors have promoted this development. Prominent French intellectuals and scholars Michel Foucault and Pierre Hadot propagated the idea of 'philosophy as a way of life' (or as the primary basis for a way of life) and as a means of taking 'care of the self'. They presented Stoic thinkers such as Seneca and Marcus Aurelius as key expressions of such ideas. Other well-known scholars, including Martha Nussbaum, drew attention to the idea of the therapy of emotion in Hellenistic philosophy, especially Stoicism, and to the idea of philosophy as a basis for the management of one's emotions.

A different kind of factor has been the emergence of CBT (cognitive behavioural therapy) as a widely used form of psychotherapy, especially in the UK and USA. By contrast with psychoanalysis, for a long time the most influential form of psychotherapy, CBT is directed at enabling people as agents to address and change their beliefs and actions, consciously and deliberately, rather than at uncovering the unconscious roots of mental disorder. In this respect, CBT is much closer to ancient philosophical forms of ethical guidance and emotional therapy, including Stoic versions of these. Stoic writings, especially certain ideas in Epictetus, were influential on early exponents of therapies of this kind, notably Albert Ellis. In turn, CBT therapists with a committed interest in Stoicism, such as Donald Robertson, have been active in using Stoic ideas as a source of life-guidance.

Several central features of Stoic ethics stressed in this book have rendered Stoicism especially suitable as a basis for life-guidance. One is the emphasis on our scope as agents for determining our own happiness, through the development of virtue, regardless of the external circumstances of our life. Another is the belief that all human beings are essentially capable of developing towards virtue and virtue-based happiness, and of doing so through activities that form part of a normal human life. This is linked, in turn, with a view of ethical development as a function of adult life, and one that can persist throughout one's life, not a process that belongs primarily to childhood and youth.[8]

Also important is the Stoic view that emotions and desires are shaped by beliefs and are open to change through changes in belief; the Stoic therapy of emotions is based on this assumption.[9] Another highly significant factor, linked with Stoic ideas about ethical development is the presence of extensive writings of guidance on, for instance, practical decision-making, gift-giving and other expressions of generosity, and emotional management. Also, Seneca, Musonius Rufus, Epictetus and Marcus Aurelius offer the kind of generalized advice, relating to our whole way of life, we associate with 'life-guidance'.

A further factor is the formulation by Stoic thinkers of programmes enabling people to shape their own patterns of behaviour and attitudes, presented as three stages or aspects. Seneca's programme consists of: (1) assessment of value; (2) adjustment of motivation to the results of assessment; and (3) achieving consistency between motivation and subsequent action. Epictetus' programme centres on: (1) examining desires and aversions; (2) shaping motivation directed at appropriate actions, especially those linked with social relationships; (3) exercising care and consistency in judgements.[10] Pierre Hadot, especially, has placed great emphasis on the significance of Epictetus' programme, seeing it as underlying the kind of ethical guidance offered by both Epictetus and Marcus Aurelius.[11] This programme has also sometimes been used as a basis for modern life-guidance.

MODERN STOIC LIFE-GUIDANCE AND EXERCISES

These features of Stoic ethical thought have served as a source of inspiration and resource for those offering life-guidance through books, online courses and events aimed at a broad public audience. There is now a large body of Stoic life-guidance, which is very widely used. In illustrating its methods, we focus on Modern Stoicism, a movement in which both the authors of this book are actively engaged. Formed in 2012 as a collaborative project involving Stoic scholars, psychotherapists and 'life-coaches' or writers, this organization focuses on three main activities. These are: (1) an edited blog of articles on applying Stoic principles in one's life ('Stoicism Today'); (2) regular one-day conferences, sometimes online, on putting Stoicism into practice ('Stoicon'); (3) an annual week-long online course, offering an introduction to Stoic practice ('Stoic Week').

Stoic Week offers a clear illustration of life-guidance. The handbook outlines the history and main features of Stoic ethics, as well as presenting the methods used in the course. Each day of the week offers material for a short period of reflection, in the morning, midday and evening. The material consists of quotations from thinkers such as Epictetus, Seneca and Marcus Aurelius, along with suggestions about how these quotations can help us to shape our actions and feelings and our relationships with others. Each day has an overall theme, such as 'character and virtues', 'caring for ourselves and others', 'seeing the big picture' (i.e. nature). It also includes at least one longer reflective or meditative exercise, typically at midday. The morning and evening reflections are focused on helping us to prepare for the day ahead or to reflect on the day past, considering whether we have put in practice the Stoic principles illustrated in the quotations.

The reflective exercises are based on themes in ancient Stoic writings on guidance and are also informed by modern (CBT) psychotherapeutic practice. Here are some examples. One theme is 'the dichotomy of control'. Epictetus repeatedly urges us to distinguish between what does and does not lie within our control, and to focus on what we can determine by our own actions. This theme reflects the Stoic claim that our happiness in life depends on our agency, and on using this to develop virtue, rather than on things such as health and property, that is 'indifferents' (which Epictetus calls 'externals'). Epictetus stresses that failure to focus on what we can control leads to pointless emotional distress as well as misdirection of our energies.

Another exercise is 'values-clarification', designed to promote reflection on what matters most to us and on whether we are putting our principles into practice. This exercise is sometimes used in CBT therapy; but in this context, it functions as a starting point for reflecting on Stoic ideas about the difference in value between what is really good (virtue and what depends on virtue) and other things often seen as good, which Stoics describe as 'indifferents'. The virtue–indifferents distinction is quite difficult to grasp and put into practice; and this exercise forms a way of helping to make sense of it.

The Stoic Week handbook stresses that the Stoics regard care for oneself and for others as core human motives. It recognizes that care for others is normally directed to family-members and those who form part of our community. However, it also underlines the Stoic emphasis on working towards extending the boundaries of our concern to those falling outside our community, and the idea that all human beings, as rational and sociable animals, form a broad family or fellowship. For this purpose, an exercise is based on Hierocles' guidance on contracting the circles of our relationship, and extending the boundaries of our concern, in principle, to any given human being.[12]

The handbook also brings out the point, made forcefully by Epictetus, that our emotions are not responses to events, but to our beliefs about events, particularly beliefs about what is good or bad. This forms a bridge to explaining the Stoic view that ethical development has an emotional dimension, and that emotions, like actions, are 'up to us', in that they fall within our agency and can be modified by reflection. One exercise used in this connection, based on Stoic writing on the therapy of emotion, is 'preparation for disaster' by imagining it in advance. Part of this reflection centres on reducing our fear and anxiety by thinking in some detail about how we might react in dangerous and distressing situations. Another part lies in recognizing that such situations are not, if properly considered, 'bad', compared with becoming morally corrupt or vicious (that is, recognizing the Stoic distinction between what is good or bad and 'indifferents').

Another much-used exercise is adopting 'the view from above'; that is, imagining that we can see our own existence and situation from a cosmic standpoint and thus placing our immediate and pressing concerns in a much broader perspective. This exercise is based on Marcus Aurelius.[13] In addition to its effect on our emotions, this exercise evokes the Stoic belief that we form an integral part of nature as a whole, and that this fact can inform our understanding of key ethical concepts such as virtue and happiness. Also, given our modern situation, this exercise can be used to underline the ethical importance of action to repair environmental damage, a theme explored in Chapter 9.

An important part of the work of Modern Stoicism has consisted in assessing the effectiveness of Stoic guidance as a resource for modern audiences. Those registering for Stoic Week are invited to review its effectiveness by questionnaires. We have used three standard scales (on life satisfaction, positive and negative emotions, and flourishing); on all these scales, taking part in Stoic Week is seen by participants as bringing about significant improvements (consistently, about 15 per cent). Recent assessments have also shown that Stoic Week has a markedly positive effect in promoting the sense that one's life has meaning and purpose. We have also devised a SABS (Stoic attitudes and behaviour scale) to enable people to assess how far their attitudes and behaviour match Stoic expectations); the results on this scale correlate closely with positive results in the wellbeing scales. There are detailed annual reports on assessment (prepared by CBT therapist Tim LeBon), and assessment of this kind is ongoing, as well as research on the psychological value of Stoic guidance.[14]

More extended courses have also been prepared and used successfully by Modern Stoicism and the Aurelius Foundation, an organization with similar aims. These courses form one strand in a broad complex of activities and resources currently available for putting Stoic ethical principles into practice. The Stoic Week course and its exercises have been discussed in some detail to illustrate the kind of Stoic life-guidance currently being offered, and to bring out how this relates to the Stoic ethical ideas discussed in this book.

MODERN APPLICATIONS

When we read a book on ethics, we often have certain expectations for what we'll find: certain concepts are covered, certain terminology is used, and arguments and conclusions are presented in a certain way. In ancient Stoicism, however, ethics was often presented not as a purely theoretical system but as a framework for living: philosophy as a way of life. For this reason, Stoic ethics was often expressed through genres like letters to friends (Seneca), personal notebooks (Marcus Aurelius) and lively discussions (Epictetus), which directly encouraged and inspired the student to apply philosophical principles in their daily life.

Pierre Hadot, the French scholar who popularized the term 'philosophy as a way of life' with reference to ancient ethics, maintains that there's no clear demarcation between philosophy as theory and philosophy as practice. Rather, we can think of philosophy as an oval or ellipse with two poles, one pole for discourse and the other for action, with any given philosophical discussion falling closer to one or the other of these poles. A philosophical life will naturally integrate both poles.

The ancient Stoics frequently highlighted this close relationship between discourse and action. Epictetus, scolding a student who believed that philosophy was all about writing commentaries on the works of famous philosophers, reminded him that:

> A builder doesn't come forward and say, 'Listen to me as I deliver a discourse about the builder's art', but he acquires a contract to build a house, and shows through actually building it that he has mastered the art. And you for your part should follow a similar course of action: eat as a proper human being, drink as a proper human being, dress, marry, have children, perform your public duties ... Show us these things to enable us to see that you really have learned something from the philosophers.
>
> (*Discourses* 3.21.4–6)

While they considered theory important, of course, theory without practice (or discourse without action) would defeat the purpose of studying philosophy in the first place. Within the Stoic framework, the ultimate goal of philosophical inquiry is not merely a theoretical understanding of the world but the ability to act well within it.

In fact, the Greek and Roman Stoics often called philosophy 'the art of living', equating it to a technical art like medicine or music. Musonius Rufus, teacher of Epictetus and a famous philosopher in his own day, put it this way:

> Virtue is not simply theoretical knowledge, but it is practical application as well, just like the arts of medicine and music. Therefore, as the physician and musician not only master the theoretical sides of their respective arts but must also train themselves to act according to their principles, so a man who wishes to become good not only must be thoroughly familiar with the precepts that are conducive to virtue but must also be earnest and zealous in applying these principles.
>
> (*Lecture* 6)

Just as doctors or musicians must have a firm grasp of theory but also skilfully apply that theory to their real-world performance, so must philosophers apply their theoretical knowledge in the arena where it matters most: everyday life.

Training in practical matters is, therefore, essential for anyone claiming to practise philosophy. The ancient philosophical schools developed numerous exercises to help adherents match their practice to their principles, including group discussion, reading, meditation, memorizing key phrases, keeping a philosophical journal and identifying inspirational role models. Many of these practices were orally transmitted through each school and so do not survive today. However, the surviving writings from the Roman Stoics form the basis of the life-guidance movement described earlier, which brings practical philosophy to many people who might not otherwise pick up a book on ethics.

In this way Stoicism is very egalitarian, seeing virtue as available to a wide range of people regardless of their background, occupation, socio-economic status or access to a university education. In contrast to some other philosophies, such as Aristotelianism, which holds that a certain type of education is necessary for virtue, and which sees the intellectual life as superior to other modes of living, Stoicism maintains that anyone with the proper desire to live a good life can make real progress towards virtue and *eudaimonia*. In addition, Stoicism offers psychological resources for dealing with the individual and collective challenges that every person faces, from coming to terms with death to getting along with your family. It's no wonder Stoicism is thriving as a source of life-guidance in today's open-ended ethical landscape.

You might want to spend some time thinking about your own most pressing questions in life and whether it's important for any philosophy you adopt on theoretical grounds to provide appropriate guidance on these questions. Does it matter to you if an ethical theory is wonderfully articulated but does not offer guidelines for practical living? Does it matter if a philosophy helps only certain individuals to live a good life but excludes others?

Thinking of philosophy as a way of life or an art of living helps us to refine our philosophical priorities when we do sit down to reflect on ethics. Not only does an ethical system need to be conceptually sound; it also needs to be inclusive, psychologically credible and responsive to real-world demands. In other words, we want a philosophy that is coherent both as a theoretical system itself and as an effective guide for living a truly good life – for everyone.

Stoicism shines in all these areas. As emphasized repeatedly throughout this book, the Stoic position on nature and virtue enables it to meet the demands of everyday life while staying coherent on the theoretical level as well. By departing at key points from conventional morality, but remaining close to human and cosmic nature, Stoicism meets the theoretical and real-world challenges of philosophy as a way of life.

NOTES

1. See Chapters 1–2. A key source is Cicero, *On Ends* 3–5.
2. Russell 2012 presents the rival merits of the two theories but favours the Aristotelian approach overall.
3. See Chapter 1, p. 16, Chapter 6, pp. 89–90.
4. Aristotle, *NE* 4.2–3.
5. Chapter 1, p. 15, Chapter 2, pp. 29–30.
6. Chapter 5, pp. 74–75. Hursthouse 1999, ch. 1.
7. Chapter 7, pp. 104–106.
8. Chapter 4, pp. 56–58.
9. Chapter 6, pp. 88–89, 95–96.
10. Seneca, *Letters* 89.14, Epictetus, *Discourses* 3.2.1–5; LS 56 B–C.
11. Hadot 1995: 191–202.
12. See Chapter 7, p. 110.
13. Marcus Aurelius, *Meditations* 7.48, 9.30, 12.24.
14. John Sellars has recently set up a Centre for the Application and Study of Stoicism, at Royal Holloway, University of London, to take forward research of this kind.

FURTHER READING

Stoicism and virtue ethics:

C. Gill, *Learning to Live Naturally: Stoic Ethics and its Modern Significance* (Oxford: Oxford University Press, 2022), ch. 6, and ch. 7 (sections 1–2).

R. Hursthouse, *On Virtue Ethics* (Oxford: Oxford University Press, 1999), especially chs. 1, 8–10.

N. E. Snow (ed.), *The Oxford Handbook of Virtue* (Oxford: Oxford University Press, 2018), especially ch. 6 (Stoic virtue), and part 3 (types of modern virtue ethical theory).

On Stoicism, virtue ethics and psychotherapy:

J. Sellars (ed.), *The Routledge Handbook of the Stoic Tradition* (London: Routledge, 2016):

C. Gill, 'Stoic Themes in Contemporary Anglo-American Ethics', 346–59.

D. Robertson, 'The Stoic Influence on Modern Psychotherapy', 374–88.

Stoicism and life-guidance:

P. Hadot, *Philosophy as a Way of Life*, trans. M. Chase (Oxford: Blackwell, 1995).

M. Pigliucci, M., *How to be a Stoic: Ancient Wisdom for Modern Living* (London: Penguin, 2017).

B. Polat, *Journal like a Stoic: a 90-day Program* (New York: Zeitgeist, 2022).

D. Robertson, *Stoicism and the Art of Happiness* (London, Hodder & Stoughton, 2013).

J. Sellars, *Lessons in Stoicism: What Ancient Philosophers Teach Us about How to Live* (London: Penguin, 2022).

https://modernstoicism.com

https://aureliusfoundation.com

9

WHAT DOES STOICISM CONTRIBUTE TO MODERN ENVIRONMENTAL ETHICS?

INTRODUCTION

This chapter, like the discussion of modern virtue ethics in Chapter 8, focuses on the potential Stoic contribution to contemporary ethical debate. Here, the area involved is environmental ethics, particularly the ethical basis for an effective response to the current environmental crisis.

What is meant by 'the environmental crisis'? Primarily, we have in view the pressing threat of climate breakdown, together with global warming. This is closely linked with other environmental problems such as massive loss of animal species and plants (loss of biodiversity) and widespread destruction of forests and other natural habitats. The main cause of climate breakdown is, as is generally recognized, the release of CO_2 emissions into the atmosphere, especially from extensive use of fossil fuels such as coal and oil. Other types of environmental damage have various causes. But the predominant factor is the exploitation of natural resources to serve the needs of human beings, a process promoted by the recent huge increase in the human population, relative to other forms of life.

Obviously, these are modern problems, and those responsible for creating them are, primarily at least, human beings living now and in the recent past. Thus, it is not immediately clear how ancient Stoic ethics can help us deal with them.

However, there are two reasons for referring to Stoicism in this connection. First, Stoicism and other ancient philosophies, along with Christianity, have sometimes been held indirectly responsible for this crisis, by promoting worldviews which give exceptional status and value to human beings. Therefore, we need to consider how far the Stoic viewpoint is 'anthropocentric' in this way, and, if so, what modifications to their viewpoint are needed to enable it to make a constructive contribution to modern debate on this problem. Secondly, even though the current environmental crisis was unknown to the Stoics, their ethical outlook can be helpful for us moderns in constructing alternatives to our own, contemporary standpoint and thus forming a better approach to the environment.

Three aspects of Stoic thought are considered for this purpose. One is their ethical framework, particularly their distinctive ideas of happiness as 'the life according to nature' (meaning, in part at least, universal or cosmic nature) and the community of humankind. The second aspect is Stoic thinking on the natural world, especially as presented in their writings on theology, the main ancient source for their worldview. Thirdly, we consider the anthropocentric dimension of Stoic thought, which, on the face of it, is problematic from an environmental standpoint. We consider what modifications can be made to enable their ideas to make a positive contribution to current environmental debate.

THE STOIC ETHICAL FRAMEWORK: HAPPINESS AND UNIVERSAL NATURE

In recent philosophical discussions of environmental ethics, thinkers have drawn on a wide variety of theories to construct arguments and frameworks supporting effective environmental action. These theories have included modern virtue ethics, with contributions from thinkers such as Rosalind Hursthouse. As brought out in Chapter 8, Stoicism, like some modern theories, combines virtue ethics and eudaimonism with giving a significant ethical role to the idea of nature. For instance, a standard Stoic account of happiness is 'the life according to nature', and the kind of nature involved includes cosmic or universal nature as well as human nature. The underlying idea seems to be that human happiness and universal nature have shared characteristics, including order and consistency and (at the cosmic level) providential care.[1]

This aspect of Stoic thought is potentially important for modern environmental ethics. Of course, the Stoic idea of universal or cosmic nature is broader than 'the environment', as now understood; however, it includes the natural world or environment. Hence, we can see the Stoics as making a direct connection between happiness, understood as the best possible human life, and living in a way that brings us into harmony with the natural world or environment. The implication is that our happiness is not just a matter of leading the best possible human life but also living in a way that takes account of the proper place of human beings within the natural world. Transposed into modern environmental terms, the Stoic conception of the happy human life gives a central role to living in a way that matches the needs of the natural environment; that is, living sustainably.

The environmental implications are not limited to the overall idea that happiness consists in living according to nature as a whole. The characteristics seen by the Stoics as shared by human beings at their best and the natural world also have potential environmental significance. One set of shared characteristics is that of structure, order, wholeness and consistency, seen as common to the natural world and to human virtue and happiness. Another linkage is between nature's providential care for all aspects of the universe and human care for oneself and others (a linkage highlighted in Stoic writings on development as 'appropriation').[2]

These points have a potential bearing on modern environmental ethics. The ancient Stoics believed that human virtue and happiness are marked by inner order and coherence and are also in line with the order and coherence of the natural world. Transposed to the modern context, sustainable living can be seen as the expression of this coordination of inner and outer order and coherence. When we live in a sustainable way, our objectives and desires are shaped by the virtue of moderation or temperance and are ordered in this sense. They are also ordered in that they are consistent with maintaining the order in the natural world. Human exploitation of nature, by contrast, can be seen both as stemming from inner disorder (the absence of moderation or temperance) and as promoting disorder at the environmental level, in the form of global warming and climate breakdown, an idea explored further later in this chapter.

Secondly, in Stoic theory, the exercise by human beings of care for ourselves and others is seen as an expression of nature's providential care for the world. Recast in terms of the modern environmental debate, we can say that human care for ourselves and others needs to be exercised in a way that is consistent with nature's providential care for the world. Nature can only exercise its providential care properly (maintaining the proper balance of heat and cold in the biosphere, for instance) if we, human beings, care for ourselves and other people in a way that is compatible with maintaining the order in nature by working to limit the current rise in global warming.

THE STOIC ETHICAL FRAMEWORK: COMMUNITY OF HUMANKIND

A second feature of the Stoic ethical framework that has special relevance for environmental ethics is their distinctive idea of the community of humankind (or 'cosmopolitanism'). This idea has been noted quite often in this book, for instance, in connection with ethical development, understood as 'appropriation'. The Stoics sometimes subdivide appropriation into two strands: the development of ethical understanding and that of interpersonal and social relationships. These two strands take their starting point from two motives seen as in-built in human beings, those of care for ourselves and for others of our kind. The full development of the second strand includes not only care for family, friends and nation, but also for humankind as a whole, seen as sharing the distinctive human features of rationality and sociability. The idea of the community of humankind is sometimes used by Stoic thinkers in connection with practical decision-making, for instance in the debate on the ethics of buying and selling discussed in Cicero, *On Duties* 3.[3]

Why is the idea of the community of humankind relevant to our response to the environmental crisis? Features such as climate breakdown and global warming are caused by the collective actions of human beings and affect all human beings, whatever their localized context and situation. The Stoics stress that we should be concerned not only with the effect of our actions on ourselves and those close to us, but also human beings in general, seen as a forming a broad community. Hierocles' exercise of 'contracting the circles of relationship' is designed to promote the widening of our concern, ultimately to include humanity in general.[4]

This idea also lends support to a relevant ethical claim we can reasonably maintain: this is that, given our current situation, making an effective response to the environmental crisis has an exceptional moral status, in relation to other kinds of ethical demand. This status derives, in part, from the fact that it affects humankind as a whole, including human beings falling outside our community or nation. Its status also derives from the sheer scale of the potential future damage. If the future of humankind as a whole (or at least human life and civilization in any form we can recognize) is under threat, other, more localized, human claims become significantly less important by comparison.

STOIC WORLDVIEW AND INTRINSIC VALUE

So far, in exploring the environmental implications of Stoic thought, we have focused on ideas that form part of their ethical framework. We now consider relevant aspects of their worldview, brought out in works on theology or worldview, such as Cicero's *The Nature of the Gods*, Book 2.

One question often discussed in modern environmental ethics is the scope of things that have intrinsic value, as distinct from the value they have for human beings. Sometimes, only human beings are seen as having intrinsic value; this view (often called 'anthropocentrism') is sometimes seen as underlying the current environmental crisis. Other approaches conceive the scope of intrinsic value more broadly.

For instance, the 'sentiocentric' view attaches intrinsic value to non-human animals, because they share with human beings the capacity for sensation, and perhaps consciousness, and pleasure or pain. A broader view again, the 'biocentric', attaches intrinsic value to all forms of life, including plants, regardless of whether or not they experience sensations. Another view ('ecocentrism') attaches special value to ecosystems; that is, collections of natural entities that make up a mutually supporting and self-sustaining ecological collective. In a broad sense, the whole biosphere, the natural environment that maintains all forms of life, can be considered as an ecosystem and thus as having intrinsic value.

Where should we locate the Stoic worldview on this question? The answer to this question is not obvious. In some respects, as brought out later, the Stoic worldview seems markedly anthropocentric. However, there are also Stoic grounds for regarding the scope of intrinsic value as being very broad, indeed extending to the world or universe as a whole.

Is this extension of value based on the criteria just noted? There is little sign that the Stoics connect intrinsic value with the capacity for sensation. However, they hold a biocentric view, in a very extended form. They regard the whole universe as a living entity, which is animated by the pervasive presence of god, seen as an energizing force in all things, and identified with *pneuma* or vital breath. The Stoics can also be seen as having an ecocentric view, in the sense that they attach value to the universe regarded as an interconnected organic system.

To make fuller sense of the Stoic position on intrinsic value and the world or universe, we need to look more closely at the criteria they use for this subject. These criteria are, in some respects, different from those used in most modern discussions, though they can still contribute positively to modern debate on the value of the environment.

REASON, PROVIDENTIAL CARE AND SYSTEM

These three themes form the main criteria for the Stoic view of the value of the natural world. Although the first two at least differ from those found in modern environmental debate, the points made by the Stoics make sense in contemporary terms and have a potential bearing on current environmental debate.

The Stoics see the universe (or the world) as a whole as having intrinsic value. The universe is regarded as good in itself, and indeed as a model of goodness. Its goodness is based on its rationality or reason (*logos*). How is this rationality manifested? Rationality, in Stoic thought, is not seen as expressed only in human reasoning.

Rationality is expressed in structure, order, coherence and wholeness in any context.

For instance, the Stoics see rationality as manifested in the regular patterns of movements of the sun, moon and planets in (what we call) the solar system; and in other natural patterns, such as the lunar cycle, the cycle of day and night, and the annual cycle of the seasons. These patterns are seen as making up a coherent system or whole; and this system is regarded as 'rational' in the same sense as the system of formal logic is viewed as being rational.

Why is this system regarded, not only as rational, but also good? Goodness, in Stoic thought, is defined as what brings benefit. The order of the universe brings benefit both to itself and everything it contains, by providing a coherent and stable structure which also enables the contents of the universe to maintain themselves in a stable and structured way. Thus, the universe is seen as good and as having intrinsic value.[5]

A second salient feature of the Stoic worldview consists in their ideas about providential care. The Stoics believe that nature as a whole, conceived as immanent god, exercises providential care and concern for all aspects of the natural world. The scope of this care is very wide. It extends not only to animals, especially human beings, and plants (that is, all living things), but also to other parts of nature, including land and sea, air, the upper atmosphere, and the heavenly bodies such as sun and moon.[6] What is the overall aim of this care? The aim is to enable each natural entity to maintain itself in a stable way and to play its normal role in the broader economy of the natural world.

How is this care expressed, according to the Stoics? In living things, including plants, god or nature is present as an inner source of animation, sometimes conceived as *pneuma* or vital warmth. In animals, including human beings, nature also implants the motivation and bodily resources to enable them to survive and to reproduce and care for their offspring.[7] These forms of care enable specific types of natural entity to maintain their existence and natural character, as part of the broader natural order.

This theme reinforces the idea that the natural world has intrinsic value. The exercise of providential care for all aspects of the natural world, including living and non-living entities, implies that they have intrinsic value, quite apart from any value they have to human beings. What has value is not just the universe, considered as a rational, ordered and coherent whole, but also the full range of types of entity that form part of the natural order.

The third relevant feature of the Stoic worldview is the idea that nature constitutes an interconnected system, in which each of the different component parts contributes to sustaining the existence of other parts as well as the whole. In modern terms, the Stoics stress the idea that the world (our planet, as we call it) or the universe as a whole constitutes an interdependent ecosystem.

Here are two passages from Cicero, *On the Nature of the Gods* 2, which illustrate this idea, both in terms of the world and the universe as a whole:

> Now if plants which are rooted in the earth thrive and flourish by nature's skill, surely earth itself is sustained by the same power, for when she is impregnated with seeds, she brings forth from her bosom an abundant harvest; she embraces and nurtures the roots of plants, and makes them grow, and is herself nourished in turn by natural forces above and without. The exhalations from the earth nurture both the lower and upper air ... if the earth is sustained and nourished through the agency of nature, the same process is at work throughout the rest of the universe; plants are rooted in the earth and living creatures are sustained by inhaling the air.
>
> (2.83)

> Now the elements are of four kinds, and as these change from one to another, the nature of the universe continues to cohere; for water is formed from earth, air from water, and the aether [upper atmosphere] from the lower air; and in turn there is the reverse process, as the lower air is formed from the aether, water from the air, and earth, the lowest element from water. Thus, the fusion of the parts of the universe is maintained by these elements, of which all things are composed, as they journey up and down and to and fro.
>
> (2.84)

Obviously, the Stoic worldview incorporates ideas such the four elements (earth, air, fire, water) which are completely outdated. However, the idea conveyed in both these passages that the world and universe form an interconnected ecosystem is wholly compatible with modern scientific worldviews.

THE STOIC WORLDVIEW AND ENVIRONMENTALISM

How do these Stoic ideas relate to modern environmental ethics and how can they contribute to modern debate? They bear on the question of what parts of nature have intrinsic value. The Stoic worldview, in two main ways, presents the idea that the world and universe have intrinsic value, apart from the value they have for human beings. The Stoic viewpoint constitutes a broad version of the biocentric one, in that the Stoics see the universe as a living entity. In another way, the Stoic worldview is an ecocentric one, which allocates intrinsic value to natural systems or complexes, rather than specific kinds of entity. These features of Stoic thinking have special relevance for two current environmental problems: loss of biodiversity and climate change, linked with global warming.

We are now experiencing a massive loss of biodiversity, both in forms of plant life, especially forests, and in types and abundance of all forms of animal, bird and insect life, apart from those used to feed human beings. From an environmental standpoint, this is problematic in two ways. The forms of life lost have their own intrinsic value (seen from a biocentric standpoint). Also lost is the contribution of these species to the natural world, considered as an interconnected and interdependent system (viewed from an ecocentric standpoint). The Stoic worldview reinforces both of these concerns, and provides its own, visionary and powerful, expression of these ideas.

The ecocentrism of the Stoic approach makes it especially effective as a means of illustrating climate breakdown and underlining the threat to the stability of the world as well as the dangers for human life. Stoicism recognizes the intrinsic value (goodness) of natural systems; and climate breakdown represents a reversal or collapse of what the Stoics present as goodness in nature. Stoicism stresses precisely those features of the natural environment (regular natural patterns and cycles, including those of climate, interdependent ecosystems, the internal coherence and connectedness of the natural world) that are thrown into danger by climate breakdown. Thus, Stoicism offers a conceptual and visionary framework that can help moderns to comprehend the scope of the damage to nature posed by global warming, in addition to the hugely damaging consequences for the future of human life.

STOIC ANTHROPOCENTRISM?

In these ways, the Stoic ethical framework and worldview makes a positive contribution to modern environmental ethics. However, there are also aspects of Stoic thought that may strike us as being anthropocentric, in a way that is problematic from an environmental standpoint. Let us examine these features and consider if they can be interpreted or modified in a way that renders them less problematic, and more consistent with the environmentally positive aspects of Stoic thought.

What are the problematic points? One is the idea that the world, or universe, is organized for the benefit of human beings, rather than other animals or plants. A related idea is that there is an in-built hierarchy in nature, and that human beings are therefore entitled to use other animals as well as other kinds of natural resources, for their own benefit. The Stoics also think that, although human beings should act justly towards any other human being, including those falling outside our own community, considerations of justice have no place in our relationships with other animals.[8] These ideas, taken on their own, run counter to modern environmental concerns and seem to justify the modern exploitation of nature by human beings that has produced the current environmental crisis.

However, on closer examination, it is not clear that the Stoic worldview should be described as anthropocentric, if this means a viewpoint that allocates value to human beings as a particular natural species, as distinct from other species or forms of life. Human beings are seen as especially valuable by the Stoics, not because they are human beings, but because they are distinctively rational, in a way that informs other aspects of their activity and experience.[9]

Also, the Stoics see the world and universe, which is shaped by embodied god, as rational. Indeed, they see the universe as embodying a higher level of rationality than human beings, because, in its totality, it constitutes a more inclusive, complex and systematic type of order than is generally found in human beings.[10] Hence, as scholars have sometimes stressed, the Stoic worldview is better interpreted as 'reason-centred', or 'logo-centric', rather than human-centred.

A MODIFIED VERSION OF STOIC ANTHROPOCENTRISM

This point opens the way to providing a modified version of Stoic thinking on the place of human beings in nature, one that is more consistent with their overall thinking. Thus, instead of saying that human beings are entitled to use other animals and natural resources for their own benefit, we should say that we are justified in treating other parts of nature *in a rational way*. And 'in a rational way' can include helping to maintain the natural order that the Stoics see as embodying rationality. This would include acting in a way that enables other animal species to maintain life and reproduce and to continue to form part of the broader ecosystem; in this way it would support the overall – rational – aims of providential nature.

Put differently, human beings should use their distinctive rationality on behalf of other (less rational) forms of life, and for the sake of the overall (rational) order of nature. This idea is sometimes described in contemporary thought as exercising 'stewardship' over nature, rather than 'dominion' over it. This kind of stewardship is, in fact, suggested by Marcus Aurelius in this passage, though it is an exceptional one in Stoic writings: 'In the case of irrational animals and objects and things in general, treat them with generosity of spirit and freedom of mind, since you have rationality and they do not' (*Meditations* 6.23). This idea is reinforced by reminding ourselves of the Stoic insistence that we (human beings) form an integral part of nature and are not separate from it, and that our value as human beings is substantially less than that of nature as a whole.

CONCLUSION

Overall, then, we can see Stoicism as making a distinctive and positive contribution to modern environmental ethics. Stoicism does so partly through its ethical framework, especially the ideas of happiness as the life according to (cosmic) nature. It contributes also by its worldview, especially the idea that the natural order (seen as an interconnected 'ecosystem') has intrinsic value. Therefore, in modern environmental terms, climate breakdown constitutes the disruption of this natural order, and working to repair this damage constitutes an especially powerful kind of moral claim. Although, on the face of it, Stoicism also expresses an anthropocentric outlook, this approach can be reconceived and modified in a way that renders it consistent with the overall Stoic worldview and ethical framework.

MODERN APPLICATIONS

How can we incorporate care for the environment into a contemporary version of Stoic ethics? Because Stoicism is centred on virtue and virtuous agents, we need to integrate environmentalism into our understanding of virtue. One option for doing this would be to add another virtue (environmental care or respect for nature) to the existing canon (wisdom, justice, courage and temperance). However, this might imply that caring for the environment is separate from the other things ethical agents do, whereas we believe caring for the environment must be completely integrated into all our actions. We suggest that the best option is to incorporate care for the environment into the way we understand the four cardinal Stoic virtues. Instead of thinking of environmental responsibility as a separate virtue, it becomes part and parcel of all our virtuous interactions with the world.

One way to think about environmental virtue is by adopting the multifaceted approach Cicero uses for decision-making based on the virtues in *On Duties* 1. Cicero describes each cardinal virtue in two ways: he outlines the core character of each virtue and then explores the other-directed and socially oriented dimension of the virtue. The virtue of justice, for example, is defined in its core character as proper treatment of other people and property. But it is also expressed as a positive desire to act generously towards other people and engage positively with them in social settings such as family, friendship, and the community. The primary, all-purpose definition of justice allows us to apply it generally to many different cases, but the second description highlights the actively benevolent and other-directed aspect in our social interactions.[11]

Similarly, we might think of each virtue as having an environmental dimension in addition to its basic character (which we can designate as 'e-virtue'). For example, e-justice can include respecting and treating properly animals, plants, natural resources and the earth itself; and e-temperance can mean not taking any more from the earth than is necessary for our basic needs. When deliberating about appropriate actions, we should consider the environmental dimension of justice and temperance alongside the social dimension. In this way, environmental care is expressed through our everyday actions, just as care for other people is expressed through our interactions with them.

Let's look at two examples of how environmental virtue can be combined with the traditional Stoic virtues and incorporated in this way into everyday life:

Example 1: Eating. As the Roman Stoic Musonius Rufus noted, eating is one of our primary areas for ethical choice because, unlike some other decisions we make, we eat several times every day. Improving our approach to eating can, therefore, have a major impact on our character (as well as our carbon footprint). Musonius was concerned about mealtime as an arena for temperance or moderation, noting that 'the beginning and foundation of temperance lay in self-control in eating and drinking' (Lectures 18A). Obviously, this is still a major consideration when we eat today. We don't want our desire for food and drink to get the better of us, and we don't want to overeat and end up harming our bodies.

Today, however, we also have the environmental dimension to consider. Not only does ethical eating nourish our own bodies better, but it also shows care for the planet. For example, choosing simpler, locally grown, less processed foods is better for human health as well as environmental health. Or deciding to cook at home (rather than ordering takeaway meals) reduces packaging waste and transportation emissions, with the added benefit that home cooking is usually healthier and more economical.

In the case of our food choices, traditional virtues like moderation and self-control blend seamlessly with the environmental aspects of those same virtues.

Example 2: Hobbies. We normally don't think of our hobbies in ethical terms; they're just things we enjoy doing in our free time. But like everything else we do, hobbies fit into the bigger picture of our lives and so must align with our ethical framework. If we have time on our hands, for example, we could choose to watch movies, play video games, go shopping ... or go hiking, start a windowsill garden or just enjoy the local park.

While there's nothing wrong with occasionally enjoying consumer pursuits as a pastime, both wisdom and e-wisdom would suggest getting out into nature is a more beneficial way to spend our time. By interacting with plants, animals and the environment in a respectful way, we actively show care and appreciation for the natural world (e-justice). Several virtues are involved in the decision-making process here, and environmental care is woven into all of them.

Clearly, environmentalism as an aspect of virtue requires a shift in our mindset. Rather than thinking of environmental care as a separate strand of action, we begin to think of it as an integral part of virtue that permeates all our actions. Caring for the earth is not something we might be doing at some times and not at others, but rather something we're always doing as we go about our daily lives.

Overall, then, Stoicism provides both a theoretical and practical basis for applying e-virtue in our lives. On a theoretical level, we regard environmental concern as completely integrated into our understanding of virtue, not as a separate virtue. On a practical level, we learn to incorporate environmental thinking into ethical action more generally, not as a separate strand of action. In this way, Stoicism provides an excellent framework for bringing environmental ethics into everyday living.

NOTES

1 Chapter 1, pp. 20–22.
2 Chapter 4, p. 58, 63.
3 Cosmopolitanism and appropriation, Cicero, *On Ends* 3.62–4 (IG: 156–7): Chapter 4, p. 63; buying and selling: Cicero, *On Duties* 3.50–7 especially 52, Chapter 5, p. 80.
4 LS 57 G, Chapter 7, p. 110.
5 Cicero, *The Nature of the Gods* 2.37, 133, 154, 156–62 (IG: 66, 75, 77–8). Chapter 1, pp. 20–22.
6 Cicero, *The Nature of the Gods* 2.73–153 (IG: 69–77).
7 Cicero, *The Nature of the Gods* 2.23–5, 28–30, also 2.122–9 (IG: 63–5, 74).
8 Cicero, *The Nature of the Gods* 2.151–62 (IG: 77–8); *On Ends* 3.63–4, 67 (IG: 157).
9 Cicero, *The Nature of the Gods,* 2.133, 154 (IG: 75, 77).
10 Cicero, *The Nature of the Gods* 2.16–17, 33–4, 36–9 (IG: 21, 65, 66).
11 Chapter 3, pp. 43–44.

FURTHER READING

For more advanced study:

Ancient writings on the Stoic worldview:

Cicero, *The Nature of the Gods*, translated with introduction and notes by P. G. Walsh (Oxford: Oxford World's Classics, 1998), Book 2. (Extracts in IG: 60–78; and LS section 54).

S. Gardiner, and A. Thompson (eds), *The Oxford Handbook of Environmental Ethics* (Oxford: Oxford University Press, 2017), especially part 2 (environmentalism and value) and part 8 (climate change).

C. Gill, *Learning to Live Naturally: Stoic Ethics and its Modern Significance* (Oxford: Oxford University Press, 2022), 292–306.

S. Shogry, (2021), 'Stoic Cosmopolitanism and Environmental Ethics', in K. Arundsen (ed.), *Routledge Handbook of Hellenistic Philosophy* (London: Routledge, 2012), 397–409.

K. Whiting, A. Dinucci, E. Simpson and L. Konstantakos, 'The Environmental Battle Hymn of the Stoic God', *Symposion* 9.1 (2022), 51–68.

Also (applied Stoicism):

K. Whiting and L. Konstantakos, *Being Better: Stoicism for a World Worth Living in* (Novato: New World Library, 2021), ch. 8.

GLOSSARY

Anthropocentrism The view that only human beings have intrinsic value.
Appropriation: see *Oikeiōsis*.
Aretē Virtue or excellence bearing on someone's character and life as a whole; the quality which makes us describe someone as good or bad overall. Conceived in Stoic thought as knowledge or expertise in living.
Biocentrism The view that attaches intrinsic value to all forms of life, including plants, regardless of whether or not they experience sensations.
Care for oneself and others Conceived in Stoic thought as in-built basic, natural motives in all human beings (and other animals); fundamental to theory of *Oikeiōsis*.
CBT Cognitive behavioural therapy, a widely used form of psychotherapy based on changing beliefs and behaviour.
Cognition Modern psychological term denoting unit of intelligence, e.g. thought, perception; similar in meaning to impression (*phantasia*) in Stoic thought.
Community of humankind Stoic idea that all human beings form a single large family or community, as rational and sociable animals.

Consequentialist ethics Moral approach centred on achieving beneficial outcomes.

Cosmopolitanism Being a citizen of the universe; belief that all human beings form a single large family or community.

Courage (*andreia*) One of the four cardinal virtues in Stoic ethics, expressed in facing danger and adversity without fear for a good reason.

Daimōn Guardian spirit within each person, identified with 'mind' in Stoic thought.

Decorum Fittingness, used by Cicero as a variant of the cardinal virtue of temperance or moderation; combines management of emotions and desires with respect for other people.

Dispreferred or dispreferable indifferents Technical term in Stoic thought for things that have negative value and are naturally avoided by human beings, e.g. illness, poverty; contrasted with vice which is bad.

Ecocentrism The view that attaches intrinsic value to ecosystems.

Ethical naturalism The view that nature, in some sense, is fundamental or important for ethics.

Ēthos Character. Sometimes seen as a key factor in ethical life.

Ethos Habit or habituation. Sometimes seen as a necessary basis for virtue.

Eudaimonia Happiness or flourishing, assumed by the ancient Greeks to be the overall end or goal of life or what makes life worth living.

Eudaimonism Theory of happiness.

Eupatheiai Good emotions, experienced only by the ideal wise person.

Good Defined in Stoic thought in terms of benefit and realization or fulfilment of rational nature. Key characteristic of virtue (and things dependent on virtue), but not of indifferents.

Hēgemonikon Controlling centre of psychological experience, which corresponds to the modern brain but which the Stoics locate in the heart.

Homologia Consistency; seen by the Stoics as a mark of virtue and happiness.

Honestum Right action; a key concept in Cicero's *On Duties*.

Hormē Motive to act or react.

Human nature Conceived in Stoic thought as distinctively rational and sociable.

Indifferents Technical term in Stoic thought for things that have positive or negative value and are naturally pursued or avoided by human beings; contrasted with virtue and vice which are good and bad.

Irrationality Characteristic feature of bad emotions (passions), which are based on incorrect (or irrational) beliefs, rather than on the absence of rationality.

Justice (*dikaiosunē*) One of the four cardinal virtues in Stoic ethics, expressed in giving each person what is due to her/him and in the positive desire to form relationships and be part of communities.

Kantian ethics Kant's ethical framework, which gives a central place to duty.

Kathēkonta Actions which have a reasonable justification, including types of social actions (such as caring for family members and spending time with friends) and self-related actions (such as taking care of one's health).

Katorthōmata Perfectly right actions, performed only by a wise person.

Kosmos Universe, in Stoic thought seen as ordered and providentially organized.

Life according to nature Standard definition of happiness in Stoic ethics; alternative Stoic definitions include life according to virtue, consistency.

Logos Rationality, reason, logic or system.

Magnanimity (*magnitudo animi*) Greatness of mind or spirit; used by Cicero as a variant for the cardinal virtue of courage.

Nature (*phusis*) Key concept in Stoic ethics, identified as human or universal (cosmic) nature.

Oikeiōsis Appropriation or familiarization; seen in Stoic thought as natural process of development in animals; in human beings informed by rationality and leads towards virtue and virtue-based happiness.

Pathē The standard Greek term for emotions; in Stoic theory signifies bad or defective emotions or passions.

Persona Role; term used by Cicero to identify the four roles crucial for ethical life (human nature, individual talents and inclinations, social context, chosen projects or career).

Phantasia Impression; in Stoic theory covers both perception and thought.

Philia Friendship or interpersonal bonding.

Phronēsis Wisdom or prudence; in Aristotle, signifies practical wisdom, but, in Stoic thought, covers both theoretical and practical wisdom.

Pneuma Energizing force or vital breath, permeating the universe; identified in Stoic thought with immanent god or divinity.

Preferred (or Preferable) Indifferents Technical term in Stoic thought for things valued positively, e.g. health and prosperity and naturally pursued by human beings; contrasted with virtue, which is good.

Progress Ethical life conceived in Stoic thought as ongoing progress towards virtue and happiness for all those except the wise (fully virtuous).

Prohairesis Choice or decision involving agency and voluntary action.

Prolēpseis Preconceptions; the inborn capacity to form conceptions of key ethical ideas such as good.

Providential care Benevolent overall care, attributed to universal (cosmic) nature in Stoic thought.

Psuchē Mind, soul or personality.

Selection between indifferents Technical term in Stoic thought for rational pursuit of things valued and avoidance of things not valued; in theory of appropriation forms pathway towards virtue and virtue-based happiness.

Sentiocentrism The view that attaches intrinsic value to all creatures that have the capacity for sensation and pleasure and pain, including non-human as well as human animals.

Telos Goal of life or end, identified with happiness in ancient thought.

Temperance or Moderation (*sōphrosunē*) One of the four cardinal virtues in Stoic ethics, expressed in management of emotions and desires and respectful treatment of other people.

Therapy In Stoic thought seen as a method for treating bad emotions (passions) and converting them to good emotions through ethical development.

Things according to (or contrary to) nature Alternative technical term in Stoic thought for preferred or dispreferred indifferents.

Unity of the virtues The theory that the virtues are unified, interconnected or interdependent.

Universal (cosmic) nature Conceived in Stoic thought as characterized by structure, order and wholeness, and providential care.

Utilitarian ethics Consequentialist moral approach centred on maximizing human benefit.

Virtue Excellence of mind or character. Conceived in Stoic thought as knowledge or expertise that shapes our character and life as a whole and determines whether or not we achieve happiness.

Virtue ethics Ancient or modern moral theory centred on virtue.

Wisdom (*sophia* or *phronesis*) One of the four cardinal virtues in Stoic ethics, expressed in the desire and exercise of knowledge and sound practical judgement.

Wise person Stoic ethical ideal; proper object of aspiration for all human beings.

REFERENCES

SCHOLARLY BOOKS

Annas, J., *The Morality of Happiness* (Oxford: Oxford University Press, 1993).

Annas, J., *Intelligent Virtue* (Oxford: Oxford University Press, 2011).

Anscombe, E., 'Modern Moral Philosophy', *Philosophy* 33 (1958), 1–19.

Brennan, T., *The Stoic Life: Emotions, Duties, and Fate* (Oxford: Oxford University Press, 2005).

Fideler, D., *Breakfast with Seneca: A Stoic Guide to the Art of Living* (London: Norton, 2022).

Foot, P., *Natural Goodness* (Oxford: Oxford University Press, 2001).

Gardiner, S., and Thompson. A. (eds), *The Oxford Handbook of Environmental Ethics* (Oxford: Oxford University Press, 2017).

Gill, C., 'Stoic Themes in Contemporary Anglo-American Ethics', in J. Sellars (ed.), *The Routledge Handbook of the Stoic Tradition* (London: Routledge, 2016), 346–59.

Gill, C., *Learning to Live Naturally: Stoic Ethics and its Modern Significance* (Oxford: Oxford University Press, 2022).

Graver, M. R., *Stoicism and Emotion* (Chicago: Chicago University Press, 2007).

Griffin, M. T., *Seneca: A Philosopher in Politics* (Oxford: Oxford University Press, 1976).

Hadot, P., *Philosophy as a Way of Life*, trans. M. Chase (Oxford: Blackwell, 1995).

Hursthouse, R., *On Virtue Ethics* (Oxford: Oxford University Press, 1999).

Inwood, B., 'Rules and Reasoning in Stoic Ethics', in K. Ieradiakonou (ed.), *Topics in Stoic Philosophy* (Oxford: Oxford University Press, 1999), 95–127.

Inwood, B. (ed.), *The Cambridge Companion to the Stoics* (Cambridge: Cambridge University Press, 2003).

Inwood, B., *Stoicism: A Very Short Introduction* (Oxford: Oxford University Press, 2018).

Inwood. B. and Donini, P., 'Stoic Ethics', in K. Algra, J. Barnes, J. Mansfeld and M. Schofield (eds), *The Cambridge History of Hellenistic Philosophy* (Cambridge: Cambridge University Press, 1999), 675–738.

Inwood, B. and Gerson, L. P., *Hellenistic Philosophy: Introductory Readings* (Indianapolis: Hackett, 1997).

Inwood, B., and Gerson, L. P., *The Stoics Reader: Selected Writings and Testimonia*, translated with introduction (Indianapolis: Hackett, 2008).

Irvine, W. A., *A Guide to the Good Life: The Ancient Art of Stoic Joy* (Oxford: Oxford University Press, 2008).

Johncock, W., *Beyond the Individual: Stoic Philosophy on Community and Connection* (Eugene: Pickwick, 2023).

Korsgaard, C., *The Sources of Normativity* (Cambridge: Cambridge University Press, 1996).

LeBon, T., *Achieve your Potential with Positive Psychology* (London: Hodder & Stoughton, 2014).

Long, A. A., *Stoic Studies* (Cambridge: Cambridge University Press, 1996).

Long, A. A. and Sedley, D. N., *The Hellenistic Philosophers* (Cambridge: Cambridge University Press, 1987).

Nussbaum, M. C., *Upheavals of Thought: The Intelligence of Emotions* (Cambridge: Cambridge University Press, 2001).

Pembroke, S., 'Oikeiosis', in A. A. Long (ed.), *Problems in Stoicism* (London: Athlone Press, 1971), 114–49.

Pigliucci, M., *How to Be a Stoic: Ancient Wisdom for Modern Living* (London: Penguin, 2017).

Polat, B., *Journal Like a Stoic: A 90-day Program* (New York: Zeitgeist, 2022).

Robertson, D., *Stoicism and the Art of Happiness* (London: Hodder & Stoughton, 2013).

Robertson, D., 'The Stoic Influence on Modern Psychotherapy', in J. Sellars (ed.), *The Routledge Handbook of the Stoic Tradition* (London: Routledge, 2016), 374–88.

Robertson, D., *How to Think Like a Roman Emperor: The Stoic Philosophy of Marcus Aurelius* (London: St. Martin's Press, 2019).

Russell, D. A., *Happiness for Humans* (Oxford: Oxford University Press, 2012).

Schofield, M., 'Social and Political Thought', in K. Algra, J. Barnes, J. Mansfeld and M. Schofield (eds), *The Cambridge History of Hellenistic Philosophy* (Cambridge: Cambridge University Press, 1999), 739–70.

Sellars, J., *Stoicism* (Chesham: Acumen, 2006).

Sellars, J., *Lessons in Stoicism: What Ancient Philosophers Teach Us about How to Live* (London: Penguin, 2022).

Sherman, N., *Stoic Wisdom: Ancient Lessons for Modern Resilience* (Oxford: Oxford University Press, 2021).

Shogry, S. (2021), 'Stoic Cosmopolitanism and Environmental Ethics', in K. Arundsen (ed.), *The Routledge Handbook of Hellenistic Philosophy* (London: Routledge, 2012), 397–409.

Snow. N. E. (ed.), *The Oxford Handbook of Virtue* (Oxford: Oxford University Press, 2018).

Striker, G., *Essays on Hellenistic Epistemology and Ethics* (Cambridge: Cambridge University Press, 1996).

Vogt, K. M., 'The Stoics on Virtue and Happiness', in C. Bobonich (ed.), *The Cambridge Companion to Ancient Ethics* (Cambridge: Cambridge University Press, 2017), 183–99.

Whiting, K., Dinucci, A., Simpson, E. and Konstantakos, L., 'The Environmental Battle Hymn of the Stoic God', *Symposion* 9.1 (2022), 51–68.

Whiting, K. and Konstantakis, L., *Being Better* (Novato: New World Library, 2021).

TRANSLATIONS OF ANCIENT STOIC WRITINGS

Cicero, *On Duties*, edited and translated by M. T. Griffin and E. M. Atkins (Cambridge: Cambridge University Press, 1991).

Cicero, *On Moral Ends*, edited and translated by J. Annas and R. Woolf (Cambridge: Cambridge University Press, 2001).

Cicero, *The Nature of the Gods*, translated with an introduction and notes by P. G. Walsh (Oxford: Oxford World's Classics, 1998).

Cicero, *On Obligations*, translated with an introduction and notes by P. G. Walsh (Oxford: Oxford University Press, 2000).

Epictetus, *Discourses, Fragments, Handbook*, edited and translated by C. Gill and R. Hard (Oxford: Oxford World's Classics, 2014).

Lucius Annaeus Seneca: Letters on Ethics, translated with an introduction and commentary by M. Graver and A. A. Long (Chicago: Chicago University Press, 2015).

Marcus Aurelius, *Meditations*, edited and translated by C. Gill and R. Hard (Oxford: Oxford University Press, 2011).

Marcus Aurelius: Meditations, Books 1–6, translated with introduction and commentary by C. Gill (Oxford: Oxford University Press, 2013).

Musonius Rufus, *That One should Disdain Hardships: the Teachings of a Roman Stoic*, translated by C. Lutz (New Haven: Yale University Press, 2020).

INDEX

advantages (*utilia*): and conflict with right action 79–81; and relationship with virtue 77–9
Antipater 79–80, 110
anger 96–7, 98
appropriate actions (*kathēkonta*) 72–3; and decision-making 71–2, 73–4, 76, 78, 79, 81; and indifferents 72–3, 77–9, 79, 81; and nature, as criterion 75; and perfectly correct actions (*kathorthōmata*) 73, 74; and right action 74, 75, 78, 79–81; and virtue, as criterion 73, 75, 78–9, 81; and virtue-indifferents/advantages relationship 72–3, 78–9, 81
appropriation (*oikeiōsis*) 58; and appropriate actions 61, 63; and basic motives 59–60; and care of oneself 59–60, 60–3; and care of others 59–60, 63–4, 106–7; and development toward virtue and happiness 60–4; and love of children 58, 59, 63; and selection between indifferents 60–1, 62–3; and society 63–4; and stages of ethical development 60–4; and three-fold pattern 58–9; and universal nature (providential care) 21, 44–5, 58–9, 63
Aristo 28, 32
Aristotle/Aristotelian ethics 6–7, 111–12; contrasted with Stoic ethics 13, 16, 27–8, 30, 34–5, 36, 56–8, 106, 121–2, 122–3, 124; as influence on modern virtue ethics 120–1
Aurelius Foundation 129

buying and selling 79–80, 84–5, 110

cardinal virtues (four) 16–17, 19, 43–4, 75, 78
care of oneself and others 58–64; and altruism 105; and appropriation

44–5, 60–4; and nature's providential care 21, 44–5, 58, 59, 63; informed by rationality 60–1, 63; interconnected with development of virtue 60, 61, 63, 64, 106–7, 115–16; as pathways to virtue and happiness 45, 60–4; as pattern in nature 44–5, 58, 59, 63; as starting point for ethical development 45, 60–1, 63–4
Cato, as Stoic exemplar 77, 113
character 15–16, 24
choice/decision 30–1; *see also* decision-making/deliberation
Christianity 48
Chrysippus 7, 16–17, 32, 46, 59, 112
Cicero 8, 43–4, 60–4, 109–10; and *On Duties* 43–4, 73–81, 124; and *On Ends* 3 60–4; and *The Nature of the Gods* 2, 138, 141
Cleanthes 23, 56
cognitivism: in modern psychology 89, 95; in modern psychotherapy 95, 125
community of humankind 75, 80, 98, 109–11, 123, 137–8; and appropriation 63–4, 137; and community of the wise 112; and Hierocles' circles 110; and more localized relationships 63–4, 109–11, 114–16, 128; and two kinds of community 110–11
cosmopolitanism 109, 111
courage 17

death 98, 99–100, 108
decision-making/deliberation 71–2, 73–4, 78–9, 79–81
desire 90, 94
detachment or involvement with other people? 106–8; and Epictetus 107–8; and Seneca, *On Peace of Mind* 107–8; and Stoic emotions 107
development, ethical: distinctive Stoic features 56–8, 65–6, 71, 125–6; and emotions 92–5, 95–6, 97, 98–9; and guidance 66, 74, 126; as natural 57–8, 65–6, 66–8; and ongoing progress 58, 74; in Platonic and Aristotelian thought 56–7, 64; and programmes for self-management 126; and stages 60–4; and universalist approach 56–7, 65, 131; and wise person as model 58, 64, 66; *see also* appropriation
dichotomy of control 127
Diogenes 79–80, 110

egoism-altruism contrast: and ancient thought 104–5, 120; and Aristotle 104–5, 105–6; and modern thought 104, 119; and Stoic thought 105–6, 124
emotions: bad and good 90–2, 93–4, 96, 97; belief-based/rational 88–9, 91–2, 93–4, 99–102, 126; definitions of 89–91; and ethical development 92–5, 95–6, 97, 98–9; generic and specific accounts of 89–90, 107; and modern applications 99–102; as motives 88–9; in Platonic-Aristotelian thought 88, 100; and positive or negative attitudes towards others 93–4, 96–9, 107; and preferred indifferents 92–4, 97, 100; rational and irrational 91–2, 94–5, 97; and two-fold cause of corruption 92–3
environmental crisis: and anthropocentrism 135, 143–5; and climate change 134, 142

environmental ethics: and animals 143–4; and anthropocentric viewpoint 135, 143–5; and biocentric viewpoint 138–9; and biodiversity 142; and care for ourselves and others 137, 140; and community of humankind 137–8; and ecocentric viewpoint 138–9, 142; and e-virtues 145–6, 147; and goodness of universal nature 140, 142; and happiness as life according to nature 135–6; and human stewardship of nature 144; and inner and outer order 136–7; and intrinsic value 138, 140–2; and logo-centric viewpoint 143–4; and modern applications regarding eating and hobbies 146–7; and nature as interconnected system 141; and nature's providential care 137, 140–; and nature's rationality 139–40, 144; and plants 140–1; and sentiocentric viewpoint 138–9

Epictetus 8, 30, 53, 83–4, 116, 125, 126, 127, 130; and emotions 96, 97, 99, 128; and emotional detachment from other people 107–8

ethics: ancient and modern ideas of 119–20; four types of presentation (Stoic) 41–7, 51–4

fame/reputation 78–9
fittingness (*decorum*) 76–7
Foot, P. 49, 123
friendship (*philia*) 104

generosity 32, 76
goodness: and benefit 29–31, 33, 140; definitions of 29; as outcome of appropriation 62–3; and universal nature 140, 142; and virtue or happiness 28–9, 31, 33, 122

guidance, ethical: on decision-making 73–5; and links with ideas of ethical development 74

Hadot, P. 125, 126, 130
happiness (*eudaimonia*): in ancient thought 12; in Aristotle 11, 13, 27; definitions of 14; as fulfilment 22–3; and human nature 19–20, 43; and indifferents 32, 34–5; as life according to nature 14–15, 18–19, 20, 42, 43, 136; and universal nature 20–2, 46–7, 136

Hierocles 110, 128, 138
Hursthouse, R. 49, 74, 123, 124, 135

impartiality 109, 115; and family 115
impression (*phantasia*) 88–9, 92, 96
indifferents 30; according to (or contrary to) nature 32, 42; and ancient criticisms 34–6; and appropriation 60–1, 62–3; and Aristo's view 28, 32; and finances/financial security 36–8; and happiness 27–8, 31, 32, 35–8; preferred/preferable and dispreferred/dispreferable 28, 30–1, 32–3, 60–1, 62, 72–3, 79, 92–3, 97, 100

interpersonal and social relationships: in ancient thought 104–5; in Aristotle 104–6; in modern thought 104; in Stoic thought 105–6, 105–6, 107–9, 114–15

joy 91, 94, 98
justice 44, 76, 112

kindness 76, 78, 116
Korsgaard, C. 77

life-guidance in modern culture 124–5; and ancient Stoic guidance 126, 131–2; and CBT (cognitive behavioural therapy) 125; and intellectual background 125; and programmes for ethical self-management 126; and Stoic ethical ideas 125–6; *see also* Modern Stoicism
love (*philein*) 108

Marcus Aurelius 8, 24, 53, 98–9, 111, 128, 144
Medea, as negative exemplar 96–7; and children 96–7
Modern Stoicism 126–7; and assessment of courses 129; and care for ourselves and others 128; and CBT (cognitive behavioural therapy) 127; and emotions as belief-based 128; and Epictetus 127, 128; and Stoic Week 127; and reflective exercises 127
motive (*hormē*) 88–9
Musonius Rufus 52, 130, 146

nature (human): in a broader natural context 44–5, 52, 143; and happiness 19–20, 43; and modern applications 51–2; rational 143–4; rational and sociable 19–20, 42–4, 105, 109–10, 114 and right action 75, 76; and virtue 19–20, 42–4
nature (universal): as ethical ideal 45–7; and god 21, 45–7, 53; as interconnected system 141–2; intrinsic value 138, 140–1, 142; and providential care 21, 44–5, 46–7, 58–9, 136–7, 140–1; and rationality/order (*logos*) 20–2, 136, 139–40; and scholarly debate 40–1, 47–8
nature-ethics relationship: in ancient thought 48–9; in modern virtue ethics 49–50

philosophy: as the art of living 130–1; as a way of life 130–1, 131–2
Plato 6–7, 13, 48, 56–7, 111–12
Plutarch 59
pneuma 140
political theory 111–14; and Chrysippus 112; and Plato and Aristotle 111–12; and political context 113; and political involvement 112–13; and Zeno's *Republic* 112
psychology, human: in modern thought (cognitivism) 89, 95; in Platonic-Aristotelian thought 88, 100–1; and positive psychology 68; and psychophysical approach 89; and psychotherapy (CBT) 125; in Stoic thought 88–9, 90–2, 101–2, 125–6

rationality 60–1, 88–9; and cosmic order 20–2, 136, 139–40; as distinctive human feature 143–4; and sociability 19–20, 42–4, 105, 109–10, 114
Regulus, as ethical exemplar 35, 80–1
right action: and ethical development 62; and ethical guidance 74, 75, 79–81; and intention 82; in modern ethics 119; in modern virtue ethics 74, 124; and relationship to virtue 74, 75, 78, 79, 81, 83, 124; and rules 82–3, 85, 119

roles (*personae*), four 77, 84, 107–8; and practical identity 77

Seneca 8, 74, 110–11, 114, 126; and *On Peace of Mind* 107; and Stoic emotions 101, 107
Socrates 6–7, 13, 99
Stoic ethics: distinctive features 5–6; and earlier Greek thought 6–7; and main ideas 1–5; and main sources 7–8; and vision 1–5

temperance/moderation 16–17, 43–4, 75
therapy of emotions 95–6, 97; and Epictetus 96, 97; and Marcus Aurelius 98–9

values clarification 127
view from above 128
virtue (*aretē*) 30–1; in ancient thought 12; and appropriate actions 73, 75, 78–9, 81; in Aristotle 13; and happiness 14–15; and human nature 19–20, 42–4; and order, structure, wholeness 20–1, 46, 94; two-fold presentation (rational and sociable) 42–3, 75, 105; unity and comprehensiveness 16–17; and universal nature 20–2, 46–7, 111; and universalist approach 123

virtue ethics, modern 120–4; Aristotelian and non-Aristotelian strands 120–1; and Aristotle or Stoicism as exemplar? 121–2, 122–3; and conceptions of goodness and virtue 121–2, 123; and conceptions of nature (human and universal) 122–3; and virtue-happiness relationship 121–2, 122–3; and virtue-right action relationship 124
virtue as expertise/knowledge: and character/disposition 15; in leading a happy life 14–15; in modern virtue ethics 123; in selecting between indifferents 32–3
virtue-happiness relationship: in ancient thought 12–13; Aristotelian view 11, 13, 106, 122; and modern applications 22–5; Stoic view 13–15, 18, 19–20, 106, 122–3
virtue-indifferents distinction 27, 28–31, 122
virtue-indifferents relationship 31–4

wisdom 16, 44, 73, 147
wise person/sage 58, 64, 66, 109, 116

Zeno 7, 16, 112

Printed in Great Britain
by Amazon